A Collection of American Crystal

A Stemware Identification Guide for
Glastonbury/Lotus, Libbey/Rock Sharpe & Hawkes

Bob Page and Dale Frederiksen

Company histories written by Pat Thompson

Published Resources:
>   Libbey Glass, Pictorial History & Collectors Guide
>   by Carl U. Fauster, Published by Len Beach Press ©1979

>   The Hawkes Hunter - T. G. Hawkes & Co. 1880-1962
>   by Bettye W. Waher ©1984

>   Stems by Concetta Emanuele
>   Olive Tree Publications ©1970

Published by Page-Frederiksen Publishing Company
Greensboro, NC

Sales Agent: Replacements, Ltd.
Greensboro, NC

Front Cover (From Left):
Strawberry, Diamond & Fan - Hawkes
Denbeigh - Libbey/Rock Sharpe
Villars - Libbey/Rock Sharpe
Jenifer - Glastonbury/Lotus
Bird of Paradise - Glastonbury/Lotus
Marina - Libbey/Rock Sharpe
Coronet - Hawkes

Back Cover (From Left):
Roseate - Glastonbury/Lotus
Chantilly - Hawkes
Martha - Glastonbury/Lotus
Manor - Hawkes
Louise - Glastonbury/Lotus
Romance - Libbey/Rock Sharpe
Chantilly - Libbey/Rock Sharpe
Vernay - Hawkes

Additional copies of this book
may be ordered from:

Replacements, Ltd.
1089 Knox Road
PO Box 26029
Greensboro, NC 27420

1-800-562-4462

@ $24.95 per copy.
Add $2.00 postage and handling

Crystal: Yodel by Lotus
China: Fiesta (Rose) by Homer Laughlin
Flatware: Daffodil by International Silver Company (Silverplate, 1950)

Crystal: Marina by Rock Sharpe
China: Bridal Rose by Spode
Flatware: Les Six Fleurs by Reed & Barton (Sterling, 1901)

Crystal: Delft Diamond by Hawkes, Stem 7227
China: Tonquin - Ruby by Wedgwood
Flatware: Francis I by Reed & Barton (Sterling, 1907)

* HAWKES

Contents

Acknowledgements

Through the cooperation and help of many friends and glass enthusiasts we were able to combine the many designs of these glass companies into our third identification guide on crystal stems and patterns. We sincerely appreciate all who enabled us to gather as much information as we have, whether supplying us with information on patterns or helping with historical data - we thank you.

Our research has allowed us to meet many people who would like to see "their" glass made into a book. We thank each of you who had a part in the finished volume.

Thanks to Jerry Reidy, Dean Six, William Parrish, Beverly Rosenow, Mrs. Gordon Rountree, Miki Fredrickson, Diane Douglass, Richard Turner, Maija Eads, Joyce Stanton, Joanne Miller and Robert Friedrich, for helping with pattern identification and supporting literature. A special thanks is extended to Don Hanse and the people of the Lotus Glass Company for supplying historical and pattern information covering their wares.

Foreword

Libbey/Rock Sharpe, Glastonbury/Lotus, and Hawkes are all glass firms with histories of producing some of the finest glassware in America. We have divided the book into three main sections, highlighting the stemware patterns of each company.

This book was designed for the purpose of making research as easy as possible. In each of the three sections, we have included a brief history of the company, a section showing the various stem shapes that we have been able to document, and the patterns as they appear on these various blanks.

In this volume we have depicted patterns that have never been shown together. This is not a completed volume of all of the patterns that each company created. We know that other patterns in each company exist that we have not been able to document and therefore have not shown. We show other patterns that we were not able to verify the cutting or pattern name. These are pictured here for cataloging purposes.

In the first part of this book, we show the stemware products of the Glastonbury and Lotus glass companies of Chicago, Illinois and Barnesville, Ohio. Lotus Glass acquired the Glastonbury company around 1960, therefore their products are shown together. These glass houses were decorating firms only, buying their blanks from other companies and applying their own designs.

In the second section, the companies of Cataract-Sharpe of Buffalo, New York, and Libbey of Toledo, Ohio, are combined. The emphasis on the pictured glassware is that of the Rock Sharpe line, from its years in Buffalo through its acquisition by Owens-Illinois, becoming part of the Libbey division. Some of the patterns and lines which were made solely by Libbey are also shown, however this book does not attempt to show all patterns that Libbey Glass has made. Cataract-Sharpe also used blanks purchased from other companies.

The last part of this book deals with the patterns that the T. G. Hawkes Glass Company of Corning, New York, produced. The illustrations shown can hardly compare with the intricate cuttings that this company produced. For most of its history, the blanks used by Hawkes were produced by other manufacturers, meeting its strict standards of quality.

The accuracy of the pattern depictions shown in this volume may vary from the actual piece. These variances are due to the source of the pattern, whether it was created from an advertisement, photograph, rubbing, or by having an actual piece in hand.

We hope you find this book useful and wish you success in identifying your glass.

A Collection of American Crystal

The Stems & Patterns of Glastonbury/Lotus, Libbey/Rock Sharpe & Hawkes

Glastonbury/Lotus

The Lotus Cut Glass Company was incorporated in Barnesville, Ohio in 1912 by some local businessmen. The company began as a small cutting operation, but by the 1920's had expanded into other decorating arenas. The firm name was changed to The Lotus Glass Company in the mid-20's. The company is still in business, presided over by Donald Hanse.

Lotus Glass and the Hanse family have been closely associated thoughout most of the company's history. Donald Hanse is the grandson of one of the first employees of the firm, glass cutter Matthew Hanse, who joined Lotus in 1913 as plant superintendent. He later became plant manager and a stockholder and acquired control of the Lotus Company after World War II. When he died in 1968, his son, Francis, who joined the firm as a salesman in 1938, became president.

No glassware has ever been made at Lotus. Over the years, the company bought undecorated stemware and accessory pieces from other manufacturers and then applied their own hand decorated designs to these items. Lotus never made any glass partly because of its close proximity to many major glass manufacturers.

"Lotus was located near at least a dozen large glass companies at one time. It was easier and cheaper to purchase ready-made items," says Donald Hanse. In the 20's and 30's, some of the firms Lotus purchased blanks from included Fostoria, Heisey, Cambridge, Duncan and Miller, Paden City Glass and Bryce Brothers.

Many older Lotus designs were based on, or made to match, Syracuse China patterns. The Syracuse China Company, based in Syracuse, New York, was a major manufacturer of fine dinnerware for many years. The company now only makes restaurant china. "Historically, crystal patterns have been based on china patterns," says Hanse.

The talented craftsmen at Lotus applied a wide array of lovely finishings to their products. Some items were hand painted. Many other pieces were encrusted with gold, silver or platinum. The rich metal banding was a trademark of Lotus.

For many years, the Lotus company concocted its own 22 Karat and 24 Karat gold for decorating. "It had a distinguishable, rich color characteristic. Other companies couldn't duplicate our coloring," says Hanse: Lotus stopped making the gold in 1980 when the long-time employee who mixed the gold died.

"Also, around that time, the EPA (Environmental Protection Agency) came out with new rules and regulations pertaining to usage of gold for decorating, so we just felt it would be better to get out of that aspect of the business altogether," added Hanse.

In the glass cutting department, employees used a mitre-cutting technique to create decorative Lotus designs.

Glastonbury/Lotus

In the past, Lotus artisans applied both light and heavy-cuttings to glass. The light-cuttings often consisted of a single flower or simple border design. Heavy-cuttings included more involved patterns, acid-etchings and often cuttings on the stems. The Lotus company is one of the last companies in the country that still applies delicate acid-etched decorations to glassware. The firm also makes its own steel plates for etchings.

Lotus Glass enjoyed its heyday in the 1940's and 1950's when it employed well over 100 workers. Outlets for the exquisite Lotus glassware included the finest of retail stores across the country, such as Macy's, Marshall-Field, Gimbel's, Jordan-Marsh, Foley's, Lazarus and Peacock Jewelers. Lotus' ware was also sent to Canada, Alaska and Puerto Rico.

In the 70's, when imports began to take over, Lotus shifted its focus to filling special orders for organizations such as the Mason's and hotels including the Hilton, Waldorf-Astoria and Ritz Carlton. The single largest order Lotus ever produced was for the opening of the Ritz Carlton in Chicago many years ago. For the occasion, thousands of stems, tumblers and barware were decorated with the hotel's lion-crest logo.

Over the years, hundreds of Lotus patterns have been made. Two of the company's most popular patterns have been the Rambler Rose #110 series and Minton #118. At one time, Lotus also imported bone china from Bavaria and decorated it with these patterns. A 100-piece china set of each pattern sold for $155.25; a 52-piece set went for $83.50. The china was sold at various department and jewelry stores. Many years ago, the Lotus company was also the sole distributor in this country of Royal Blue Delft pottery out of Holland.

More recently, a top seller for Lotus was its "Black Gold" barware, which was especially popular in the state of Texas during the oil boom of the 1980's. The pattern rose to prominence when it was featured on the CBS television series, "Dallas." Donald Hanse says he used to watch that show every week. "I got tickled when I saw J.R. drinking from Black Gold glasses."

About 1960, Lotus purchased The Glastonbury Company, a glass decorating firm out of Chicago, Illinois. Lotus bought Glastonbury's cutting machines and warehouse, and combined crystal lines and weeded out duplicate patterns. According to Donald Hanse, "Glastonbury was predominantly a cutting operation. They threw in a few etched patterns to add some spice." Unfortunately, very little is known about this firm because a 1976 warehouse fire at Lotus destroyed nearly all the records and written accounts of the Glastonbury company.

Today, Lotus Glass Company does about 25% of the cuttings that it used to do and employs a dozen people. A majority of the employees have been with the firm 20 to 50 years. Some Lotus patterns can still be found in fine jewelry stores across the country. ⫙◎⫙

Top Photo: Ralph Wilson and Wilbur Cordner applying metallic trim.
Bottom Photo: Factory overview of the glass cutting department.

Glastonbury/Lotus
Stems by Shape & Number

6
Page 9

10
Page 9

18
Page 9

19
Page 9

21
Page 9

22
Page 10

23
Page 10

24
Page 10

25
Page 11

25 opt
Page 11

26
Page 11

27
Page 11

28
Page 11

29
Page 12

35, 3848
Page 12

36
Page 12

37
Page 13

39 (a)
Page 13

39 (b)
Page 14

40
Page 14

42
Page 14

46
Page 14

51
Page 14

54
Page 15

55
Page 15

58
Page 15

61
Page 15

65
Page 15

66
Page 16

67
Page 16

73
Page 16

74
Page 16

75
Page 16

76
Page 17

77
Page 17

78
Page 17

79
Page 18

80
Page 18

81
Page 18

85
Page 18

86
Page 18

87
Page 19

88(a)
Page 20

88(b)
Page 20

89
Page 20

90(a)
Page 20

90(b)
Page 20

92
Page 20

93
Page 21

94
Page 21

95
Page 21

96
Page 22

97
Page 22

98(a)
Page 22

98(b)
Page 22

99
Page 22

357
Page 23

450
Page 23

470
Page 23

470 opt
Page 23

500
Page 23

520
Page 23

553
Page 24

682
Page 24

896
Page 24

898
Page 25

934
Page 25

965
Page 25

969
Page 25

971
Page 25

980
Page 25

981
Page 26

982
Page 26

983
Page 26

984
Page 26

1000
Page 27

1124
Page 27

1125
Page 27

1500
Page 27

3720
Page 28

7695
Page 28

D6
Page 28

L11
Page 29

L13
Page 29

L15
Page 29

L17, 333
Page 30

L18
Page 31

L22
Page 31

L25
Page 32

L26
Page 32

L31
Page 33

L32
Page 34

L36
Page 34

L38
Page 34

L39
Page 34

L40
Page 35

2000
Page 35

2001
Page 36

2002
Page 36

2003
Page 36

2004
Page 36

2005
Page 37

2006
Page 37

2007
Page 37

2008
Page 37

Stem #'s 2000 through 2008 are not factory assigned numbers, but were assigned by the authors for reference purposes.

Glastonbury/Lotus

In this 1934 photo, employees are in the process of acid etching designs on the stemware. Left and top right: Examples of McGuire design.

Glastonbury/Lotus

Stems by Pattern & Number

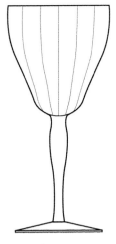

Stem 6

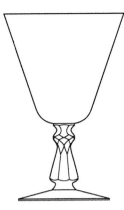

Helen
Cut 1124H
6

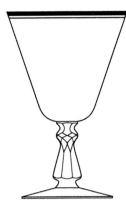

Princess
Stem 10

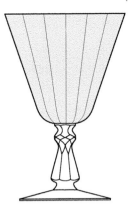

Chalet
Gold or Platinum Bands
10

Contemporary
Green Bowl, White Stem
10

Falling Leaves
Cut
10

Garden Rose
Cut
10

10-1
Cut
10

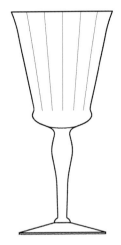

Stem 18
Optic

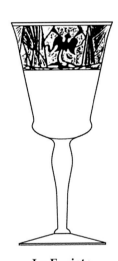

La Furiste
Gold Encr. 907, Stem 18
Rose, Green, Amber, Crystal

La Furiste
Etched 908, 2 Gold Bands
Rose, Green, Crystal, Stem 18

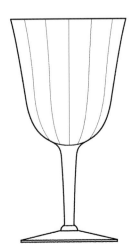

Stem 19

Florence
Cut 49
19

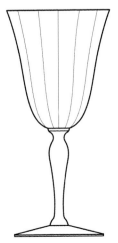

Stem 21

Decoration No. 889
Stem 21, Crystal Bowl/Rose
or Green Stem & Foot

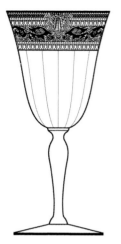

Decoration No. 902
Stem 21, Crystal Bowl/Rose or Green Stem & Foot

Grecian
Decoration No. 901, Gold Bands and Trim, Stem 21, Crystal Bowl/Rose or Green Stem and Foot

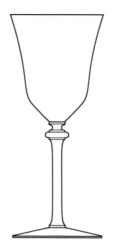

Stem 22

Decoration No. 109
Etch 1009, Gold Trim Rose, 22

Revere
Etch 1009, Rose 22

Stem 23

Cut 15
All Rose or Green 23

Dorothy
Gold Encrusted 895 23

Marie
Cut 2, All Rose or Green 23

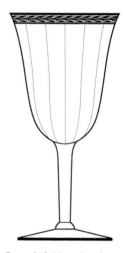

Special Herringbone
Gold Encrusted 119B 23

Special Minton
Gold Encrusted 118B 23

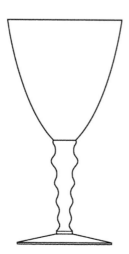

Stem 24
Crystal Bowl/Rose or Green Stem and Foot

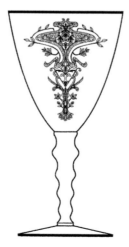

Decoration No. 109
Etch 1009, Crystal Bowl/Rose or Green Stem, Gold Trim, 24

Gene
Cut 10 24

Revere
Etch 1009, Crystal Bowl/Rose or Green Stem, 24

Stem 25

Stem 25
Optic

Gold Band 113
25

Gold Band 114
25

Improved Minton
Gold Encrusted 118
25

Iridescent Lustre
Decoration 112
25

Stem 26

Rose
Etch 1000
26

Stem 27

Yodel
Etch 1012, Crystal Bowl/Rose
or Green Stem, 27

Stem 28

Aster
Cut 42
28

Cut 36
28

Cut 37
28

Cut 40
28

Grape
Cut 12
28

Marie
Cut 2
28

Stem 29

Vine Line
Cut 38
29

Stem 35
Stem 3848

Bracelet
Gold Encrusted
35

Bridal Bouquet
Etch 0906
35

Etch 1022
3848

Grenoble
Decoration 192, Gold, Cut
35

Logan
Cut
3848

Minton
Gold Encrusted
35

Rambler Rose
Gold or Plat. Encrusted
35

Stem 36

Florence
Cut 63
36

Gold Band 113
36

Gold Band 114
36

Majesty
Cut 24
36

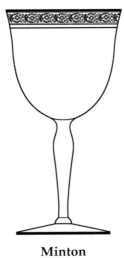

Minton
Gold Encrusted
36

Pinetree
Cut 41
36

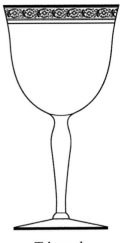

Triumph
Platinum Encrusted
36

York
Cut 740
36

Stem 37

Duchess
Cut
37

Festival
Cut
37

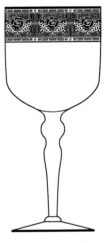

Goldenrod
Gold Encrusted
37

Lady Ruby
Cut
37

Laurel Wreath
Cut
37

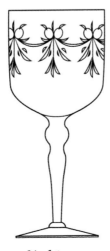

Yorktown
Cut
37

Stem 39 (a)
"Carcassone" by Heisey

Classic
Etch 1017, Sahara (Yellow)
39

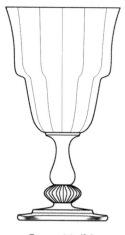

Stem 39 (b)
"Carcassone II" by Heisey

Triumph
Cut 942
39

Stem 40

Etch 1019
40

Marjorie
Cut 7
40

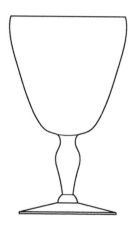

Stem 42

Cynthia
Cut
42

Dawn Rose
Cut
42

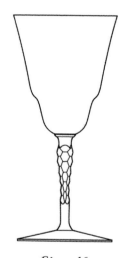

Stem 46

Olympic
Cut 16
46

Stem 51

Chantilly
Cut 25
51

Florence
Cut 63
51

Georgian
Gold Encrusted 889
51

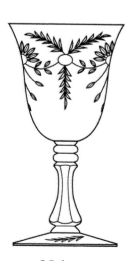

Majesty
Cut 24
51

Pinetree
Cut 41
51

Sovereign
Cut 62 1/2
51

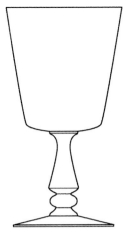

Stem 54

Dawn
Cut
54

Hardy
Cut 91
54

Windsor
Cut 47
54

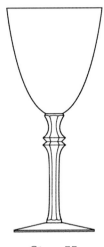

Stem 55

Sophia
Decoration 792, Etched, Gold Trim,
Stem 55, All Crystal or with Rose Bowl

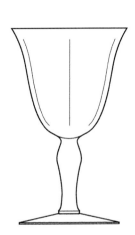

Stem 58

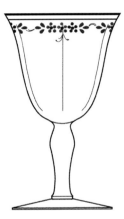

Decoration 104
Enameled, Gold Trim
58

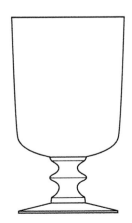

Stem 61

Celestial
Cut 47
61

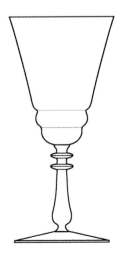

Stem 65

Florence
Cut 63
65

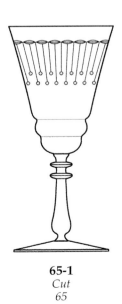

65-1
Cut
65

15

Stem 66

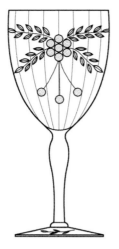

Alberta
Cut A
66

Dresden
Etch 1005, Stem 66
Crystal or Topaz

Flanders
Etch 1011, Stem 66
Crystal or Topaz

Stem 67

Empress
Cut 1
67

Hostess
Cut 17
67

Stem 73

Vesta
Etch 1041
73

Stem 74

Chintz
Cut 4
74

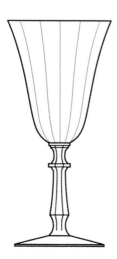

Stem 75
Optic

Decoration No. 888
Gold Design
75

Eleanor
Cut 19
75

Hostess
Cut 17
75

Louise
Etch 0796
75

Thelma
Etch 1023
75

Vesta
Etch 1041
75

Stem 76

Fuchsia
Etch 0905
76

Fuchsia
Etch 0905, Gold Encr.
Band, 76

Stem 77

Majesty
Cut 24
77

77-1
Cut
77

77-2
Gold Bands
77

Stem 78

Gold Band 0889
Etched, Two Gold Bands,
78

Golden Harvest
aka "Gold Band A"
78

Victoria
Cut 26
78

Waterford
Cut
78

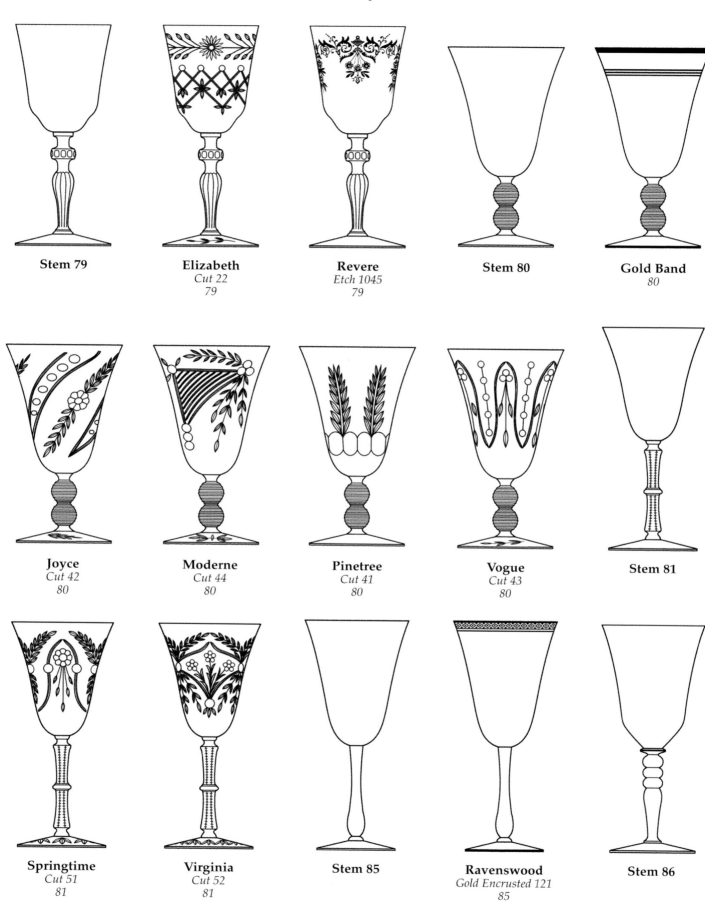

Stem 79

Elizabeth
Cut 22
79

Revere
Etch 1045
79

Stem 80

Gold Band
80

Joyce
Cut 42
80

Moderne
Cut 44
80

Pinetree
Cut 41
80

Vogue
Cut 43
80

Stem 81

Springtime
Cut 51
81

Virginia
Cut 52
81

Stem 85

Ravenswood
Gold Encrusted 121
85

Stem 86

Bridal Bouquet
Etch 0906
86

Buttercup
Decoration 0116GB,
Etched, Gold Trim, 86

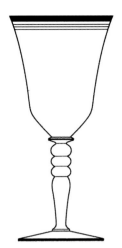

Gold Band "B"
86

Norma
Cut 8A
86

86-1
Gold Bands
86

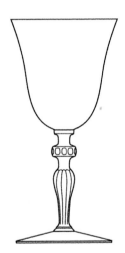

Stem 87

Bouquet
Cut
87

Hampton
Platinum Bands
87

Jenifer
Gold Encrusted
87

Ridgewood
Cut 36
87

Roma
Gold Bands
87

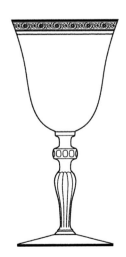

Roselyn
Platinum Encrusted
87

Serenity
Cut
87

Twilight
Platinum Trim
87

Vogue
Gold Trim
87

Stem 88

Harvest
Cut 34
88

Queen's Lace
Cut 35
88

Stem 88

Classic
Cut 48
88

Stem 89

Romance
Cut 96
89

Stem 90

Grenoble
Decoration 192, Gold, Cut
90

Regal
Cut 46
90

Stem 90

Minton
Gold Encrusted 122
90

Stem 92

Bittersweet
Cut 21
92

Colonial
Gold or Platinum Bands
92

Entwine
Cut 20
92

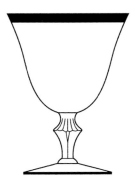

Puritan
Platinum Band
92

Wind
Cut 38
92

92-1
Cut
92

92-2
Cut
92

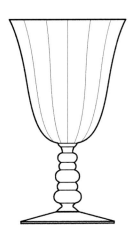

Stem 93

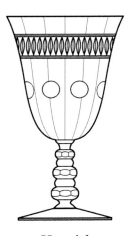

Harwich
Cut 16
93

St. Regis
Cut
93

Wembley
Cut 14
93

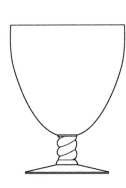

Stem 94

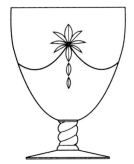

Daisy Chain
Cut
94

Mayfair
Cut 10
94

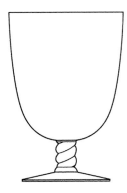

Stem 95

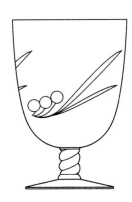

Bel-Air
Cut 45
95

Fuchsia
Cut 64
95

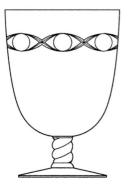

Lyric
Cut 8
95

Meadow Tree
Cut
95

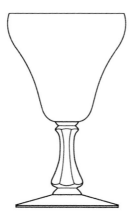

Stem 96

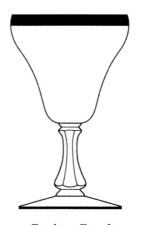

Puritan Band
Gold or Plat. Band 115
96

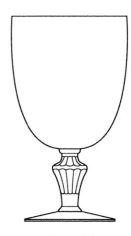

Stem 97

Cattail
Cut 49
97

Stem 98

Colonial II
Gold or Platinum Bands
98

Empress
Gold Band
98

Garland
Cut 51
98

Lotus Rose
Cut 57, Platinum Trim
98

98-1
Platinum Band
98

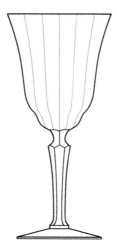

Stem 98

Bridal Bouquet
Etch 0906
98

Stem 99

Bristol
Cut 61
99

York
Cut 740
99

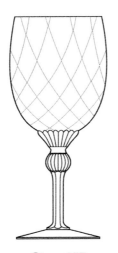

Stem 357

Mary Louise
Gold Encrusted 1008
357

Stem 450

McGuire
Etch 1001, Black Base
450

Stem 470

Stem 470
Optic

Butterfly
Etch 1014, All Crystal or
with a Topaz Bowl, 470

Louise
Etch 0796, All Crystal or
with a Topaz Bowl, 470

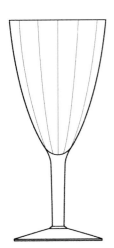

Stem 500

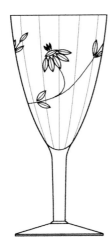

Cut 6
500

Etch 1007
500

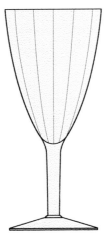

Iridescent Lustre
Mother of Pearl
500

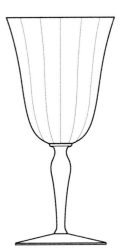

Stem 520

Martha
Etch 1003
520

Martha
Gold Encrusted 1003
520

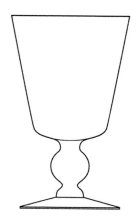

Stem 553

Caprice
Cut
553

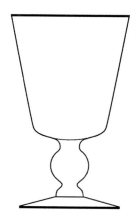

Lyric
Gold Trim
553

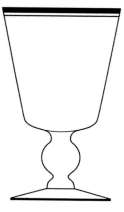

Moonlite
Platinum Bands
553

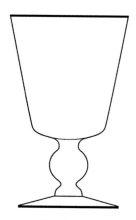

Radiance
Platinum Trim
553

Spring
Cut
553

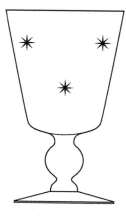

Star Dust
Cut
553

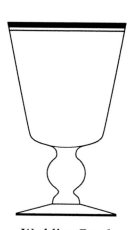

Wedding Band
Gold Bands
553

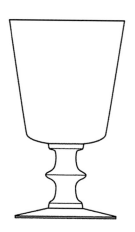

Stem 682

Hardy
Cut 91
682

Laurel
Gold Decoration 117
682

Oxford
Cut 92
682

Stem 896

Bird of Paradise
Cut
896

Stem 898

Arbor
Cut 62
898

Stem 934

Bird of Paradise
Cut
934

934-1
Cut
934

Stem 965

Chatham
Cut
965

965-1
Cut
965

Stem 969

Chantilly
Cut
969

Stem 971

Elite
Cut
971

Stem 980

Arcadia
Cut
980

Bridal Wreath
Cut
980

Stem 981

Serenade
Cut
981

981-1
Cut
981

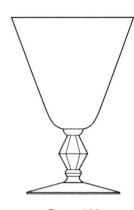

Stem 982

Arbor Rose
Cut
982

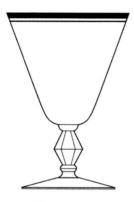

Brookmere
Platinum Bands
982

Lincoln
Gold Bands
982

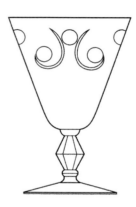

Opal
Cut
982

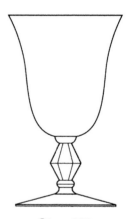

Stem 983

Citadel
Cut
983

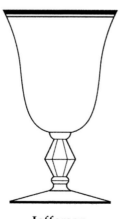

Jefferson
Gold Bands
983

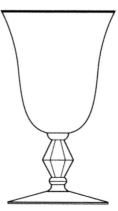

Melody
Platinum Trim
983

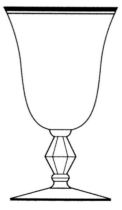

Miramar
Platinum Bands
983

Stem 984

Harmony
Cut
984

Revere
Platinum Bands
984

Rose Marie
Gold Bands
984

Stem 1000

Deloris
Cut D
1000

Stem 1124

Cosmos
Cut C
1124

Stem 1125

Minton
Gold Encrusted
1125

Rambler Rose
Gold or Plat. Encrusted
1125

Windsor
Gold Encrusted
1125

Stem 1500

Carnation
Cut
1500

Normandy
Gold Bands
1500

Vassar
Cut
1500

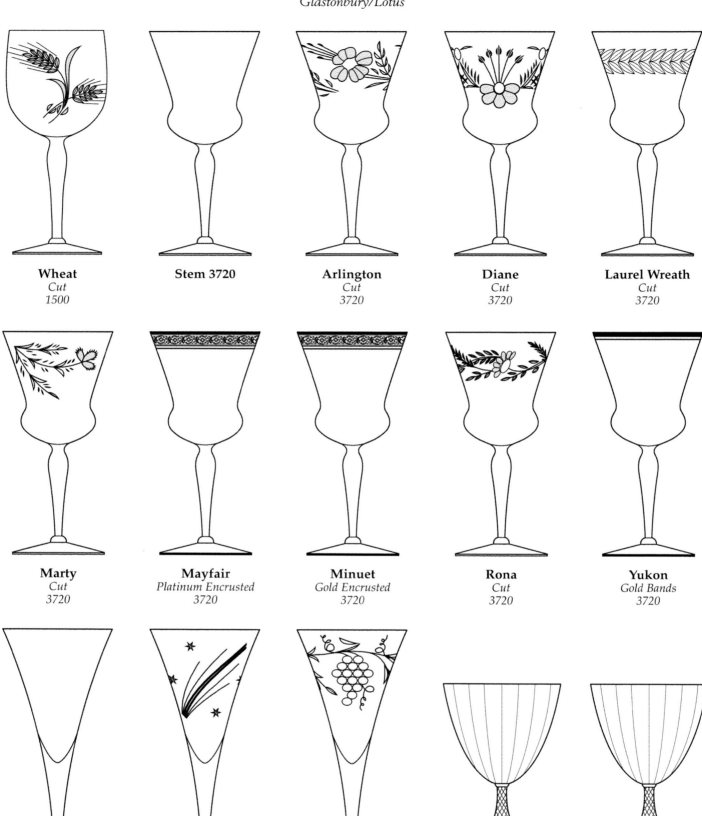

Wheat
Cut
1500

Stem 3720

Arlington
Cut
3720

Diane
Cut
3720

Laurel Wreath
Cut
3720

Marty
Cut
3720

Mayfair
Platinum Encrusted
3720

Minuet
Gold Encrusted
3720

Rona
Cut
3720

Yukon
Gold Bands
3720

Stem 7695

F-Star
Cut 32
7695

Swirl Grape
Cut 903
7695

Stem D6

Iridescent
Mother of Pearl Bowl
D6

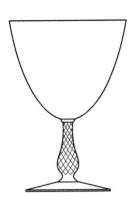

Stem L11

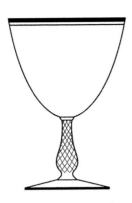

Wedding Band
Gold or Platinum Bands
"Colonial Platinum 114", L11

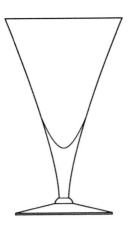

Stem L13

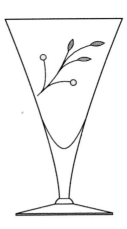

Carlton
Cut
L13

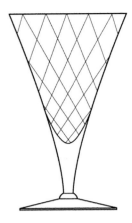

Catalina
Cranberry, Blue, Amber, or
Iridescent, L13

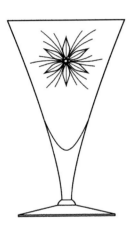

Glory Star
Cut
L13

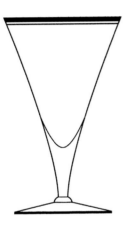

Gold Band "A"
L13

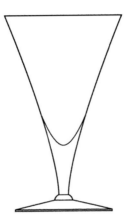

Iridescent
Mother of Pearl
L13

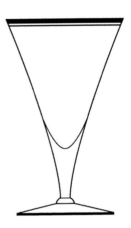

Platinum Band "A"
L13

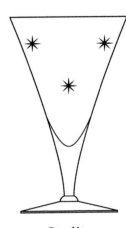

Starlite
Cut
L13

Stem L15

Colonial Platinum
Platinum Bands
L15

Deauville
Cut 19
L15

Holiday
Cut 16
L15

Nocturne
Cut 18
L15

Rose
Cut
L15

Springtime
Cut
L15

Spruce
Cut 20
L15

L15-1
Platinum Encrusted
L15

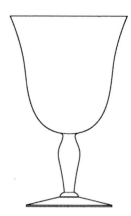

Stem L17 *Lotus*
Stem 333 *Glastonbury*

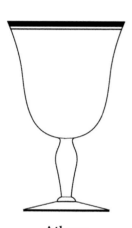

Athens
Gold Bands
L17

Carlton Rose
Cut
L17

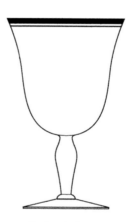

Colonial 333
Platinum Bands
333, No Trim on Foot

Flair
Cut
333

Gloria
Cut
L17

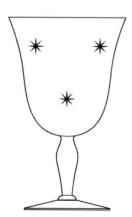

Morning Star
Cut
333

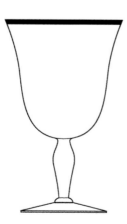

Oxford
Gold Band
L17

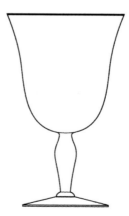

Prelude
Platinum Trim
L17

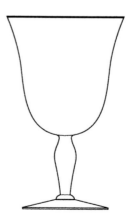

Princess
Gold Trim
L17

Priscilla
Cut
L17

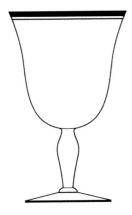

Romance
Platinum Bands
L17

Sovereign
Cut
L17

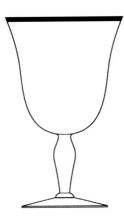

Trent
Platinum Band
L17

Wheat Spray
Cut
333

L17-1
Cut
L17

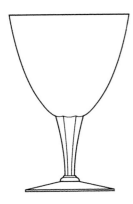

Stem L18

Elegance
Cut C-27
L18

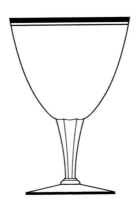

Fontana
Gold or Platinum Dec. 114
L18

Gaylord
Cut C-28
L18

Stem L22

Bride's Choice
aka "Simplicity"
L22, Gold Trim

Enchantment
aka "Palomar"
L22, Platinum Trim

Laurette
White Design, Platinum
L22

Minuet
Gold or Platinum Band
L22

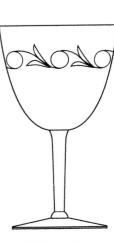

Moonglo
Cut
L22

31

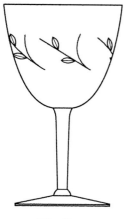

Rhythm
Cut
L22

Theme
Gold or Platinum Bands
L22

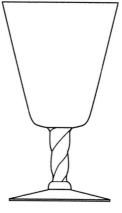

Vignette
Cut, Platinum Trim
L22

Melody
Stem L25

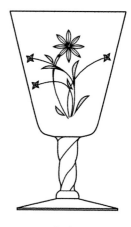

Astra
Cut
L25

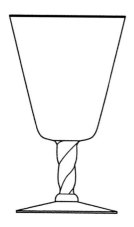

Gold Twist
Gold Trim
L25

Princess Rose
Cut
L25

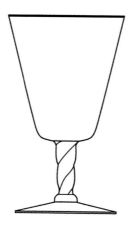

Regent
Platinum Trim
L25

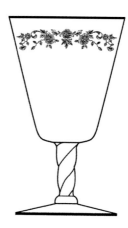

Vintage
Etched, Platinum Trim
L25

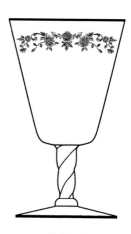

L25-1
Etched, Gold Trim
L25

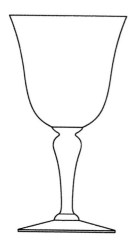

Stem L26

Arcadia
Cut
L26

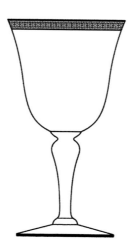

Bracelet
Gold Encrusted
L26

Cheryl
Cut
L26

Debut
Cut
L26

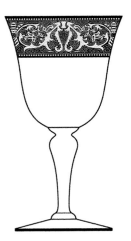

Georgian Gold
Gold Encrusted
L26

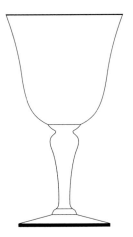

Harmony
Platinum Trim
L26

Kent
Cut
L26

Renaissance
Cut
L26

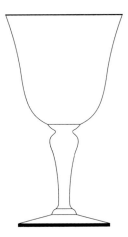

Sharon
Gold Trim
L26

Stem L31

Bridal Bouquet
Etch 0906
L31

Brocade
Etched, Gold or Plat. Trim
L31

Corinthia
Cut
L31

Cotillion
Cut, Platinum Trim
L31

Ferndale
Cut
L31

First Love
Gold Trim
L31

Flair
Cut
L31

Inheritance
Cut
L31

Rosedale
Gold Encrusted
L31

Sonata
Platinum Trim
L31

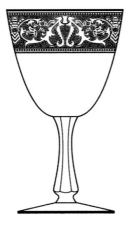

L31-1
Etched, Gold Design/Trim
L31

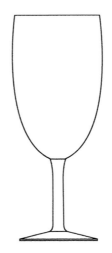

Stem L32

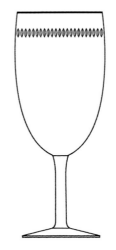

Bridesmaid
Cut, Gold or Plat. Trim
L32

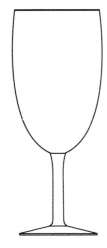

Rhapsody
Gold or Platinum Trim
L32

Roseate
Etched, Gold Inlay & Trim
L32

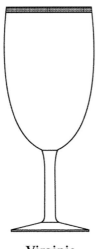

Virginia
Gold Encrusted
L32

Stem L36

Debra
Gold Trim
L36

Weatherly
Platinum Trim
L36

Stem L38

Alberta
Cut
L38

Coventry
Gold Encrusted
L38

Richlieu
Cut, Gold Inlay & Trim
L38

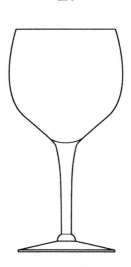

Stem L39

Florence
Cut
L39

Lenore
Gold Trim
L39

Nobility
Gold Encrusted
L39

Regina
Platinum Trim
L39

Transition
Etched, Gold or Plat. Trim
L39

Windsor
Cut
L39

Stem L40

Brookdale
Gold Trim
L40

Duchess
Cut
L40

Marlene
Cut
L40

Regal
Platinum Trim
L40

Tudor
Gold Encrusted
L40

Stem 2000

Elegance
Cut
2000

French Scroll
Cut
2000

Stem #'s 2000 through 2008 are not factory assigned numbers, but were
assigned by the authors for reference purposes.

Stem 2001

Empress
Gold or Platinum Band
2001

Stem 2002

Crest
Cut
2002

Stem 2003

Bittersweet
Cut
2003

Meadowbrook
Cut
2003

Montclair
Platinum Trim
2003

Vine
Cut
2003

2003-1
Cut
2003

Stem 2004

Celeste
Cut
2004

Cheviot
Gold Trim
2004

Empress
Cut
2004

Patrician
Platinum Trim
2004

*Stem #'s 2000 through 2008 are not factory assigned numbers, but were
assigned by the authors for reference purposes.*

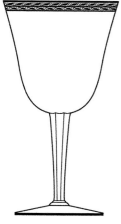

Tuxedo
Gold Encrusted
2004

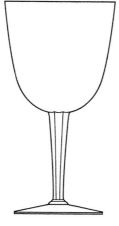

Stem 2005

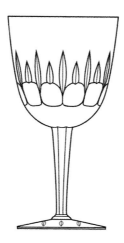

Crown
Cut
2005

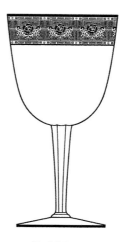

Gold Lace
Gold Encrusted
2005

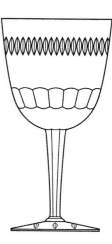

Kingsley
Cut
2005

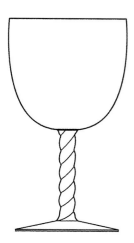

Stem 2006

Bird of Paradise
Cut, Blue Bowl
2006

Stem 2007

Exquisite
Platinum Trim
2007

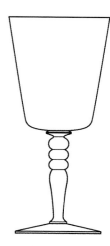

Stem 2008

Platinum York
Cut, Platinum Band
2008

Stem #'s 2000 through 2008 are not factory assigned numbers, but were
assigned by the authors for reference purposes.

Libbey/Rock Sharpe

If you had to pick two words to describe Libbey Glass Company's offerings over the years, 'diverse' and 'prolific' would certainly apply. The company has delivered such a wide array of goods: cut glass, art glass, blown glass, inexpensive hand and machine ware, pattern glass, and glassware for the hotel and restaurant trades. The list goes on!

Of course, many of these products were partly a reflection of longevity - the firm dates back to 1818 when it was originally founded as The New England Glass Company of East Cambridge, Massachusetts. The Libbey name became associated with the company through changes of ownership; William L. Libbey and his son, Edward D. Libbey, purchased New England Glass in the late 1870's, moving it to

The Libbey Trademark represented one of the world's largest producers of cut glass during the early part of this century

Toledo, Ohio in 1888. The name of the company was changed to The Libbey Glass Company in 1892.

For over a 100 years, from about 1820 to 1920, cut glass was the principal product of New England Glass/The Libbey Glass Company. In fact, Libbey was one of the world's largest producers of cut glass during the early part of this century, employing over 200 full-time engravers in 1915, leaving behind a tremendous legacy of cut glass tableware, serving pieces, and items for the home, such as vases and lamps.

These products were fashioned from expensive lead glass and engraving was done using the demanding copper-wheel technique, which is the finest and most detailed kind of engraving. Many patterns and designs were made in sets of various sizes. Today, it is common to see examples of Libbey's brilliant cut glass products on display at museums.

In the 1920's, when the popularity of cut glass began to wane, Libbey's production shifted to inexpensive hand and machine ware. "Safedge Glassware" featuring a chip-resistant rim was introduced in 1924. The Libbey Company guaranteed customers "a new glass if the rim ever chips." This glassware helped Libbey become a top supplier of wares to restaurants and hotels.

Later, there were various attempts by Libbey to revive fine glassware. For instance, The Libbey-Nash line, which was introduced in the early 30's, featured 80 patterns of hand-crafted stemware, of Steuben-like quality. The series was designed by A. Douglas Nash, a former executive with Tiffany's in Corona, New York. The luxury line was priced from $15 to $2,500 a dozen.

In 1940, when Libbey Glass was an operating division of Owens-Illinois, Modern American was introduced. This line consisted of bubble-thin table services and decorative pieces in clear crystal and colors. It was the last hand-crafted glass made by Libbey. To publicize this series, Hollywood motion picture studios were supplied with full sets of the glassware. The 1940 movie "No Time for Comedy" with Jimmy Stewart has a formal table adorned with

Libbey/Rock Sharpe

crystal in the Embassy pattern. Modern American was not made after World War II.

In the late 50's, Libbey's 1818 Line of machine made stemware was made to compete with hand-crafted patterns. 1818 Stemware was named for the year the company was founded. It consisted of automatically blown stems with the Safedge rims ground off. The bowls were cut with mitre-type designs. It was only offered for a short time in leading retail stores in major cities.

Also, in 1948, in a bid to further enhance Libbey's glass decorating capabilities, Owens-Illinois acquired the Cataract-Sharpe Manufacturing Company of Buffalo, New York, and made it a subsidiary known as Sharpe, Inc. The Cataract Company was a high quality cutting operation that decorated fine handmade stemware, tumblers and accessory pieces supplied by other firms.

For many years, Cataract-Sharpe had purchased blanks from the Libbey Glass Division of Owens-Illinois and decorated the crystal at its factory in Buffalo. Bryce Brothers Crystal and A. H. Heisey were other big suppliers of crystal for Cataract Sharpe in the 30's and 40's. The company made no glass itself.

The Cataract Company was originally formed in 1914 by Alfred H. Sharpe, who had been a manager at Fostoria Glass Company. Until 1920, the firm was known as Cataract Glass Company. Cataract-Sharpe cut many intricate, deep-cut crystal patterns. Many of the designs were ornately done and brilliantly polished. A fern-like leaf design was a very typical design for Sharpe and it appears in a variety of their cut patterns. It is important to note that the company's specific stem designs were not matched with any particular cuttings.

In the 30's and 40's, the company widely promoted its Rock Sharpe Crystal products in many of the major women's magazines. According to advertisements, the crystal was described as featuring "smart modern or rich period motifs." The stemware was sold at virtually every major department store in the country.

"Rock Sharpe was some of the best-selling stemware in America during that period," recalls Joanne Miller of Buffalo, New York, whose father, Andrew Cunningham, was vice-president of sales for Cataract-Sharpe in the 20's and 30's. "My dad also designed many of the Rock Sharpe patterns. He even designed a pattern for me." Miller says as far as she can remember, the company only decorated clear, not colored crystal.

The Cataract-Sharpe Company had extensive equipment for decorating and highly skilled cutters who employed advanced cutting and polishing methods. Until World War II, lead glass was used for Cataract-Sharpe's highest grade cut crystal glassware. The wartime shortage of lead glass temporarily intervened with Cataract's use of this product. All glass firms were required to cut back their production of glassware that was nonessential to the war effort.

After Owens-Illinois bought Cataract-Sharpe, Alfred Sharpe continued on as the President of Sharpe, Inc. R. W. Rogers, formerly a sales manager of the Libbey Glass Division of O-I, became vice-president and general manager.

In the late 40's and 50's, Sharpe, Inc. continued to produce patterns that had previously been made at Cataract-Sharpe. In addition, several new Sharpe patterns were introduced, including "Empire Wreath", "Spear and Ring", "Lattice" and "Bramble." Eventually, however, Owens-Illinois discontinued altogether the Sharpe cut crystal line.

The Libbey Glass Division is still in operation in Toledo, Ohio and has a modern plant in City of Industry, California that was built in 1962. The company is one of the world's largest suppliers of automatically-produced table glassware.

A typical advertisement used by Cataract-Sharpe Mfg. Co. in the leading magazines during the 1930's.

Libbey/Rock Sharpe

Stems by Shape & Number

Stem numbers 1001 through 3011 are not assigned by either Rock Sharpe or Libbey, but were assigned by the authors for reference purposes.

Stem numbers K11 through K9058 and the 3400 Line through the 7900 Line are actual Libbey assigned numbers.

Note: Patterns on Stems 1002 and 2002 may have been made on either stem. This occurred due to the availability of the "blank" at the date of manufacture.

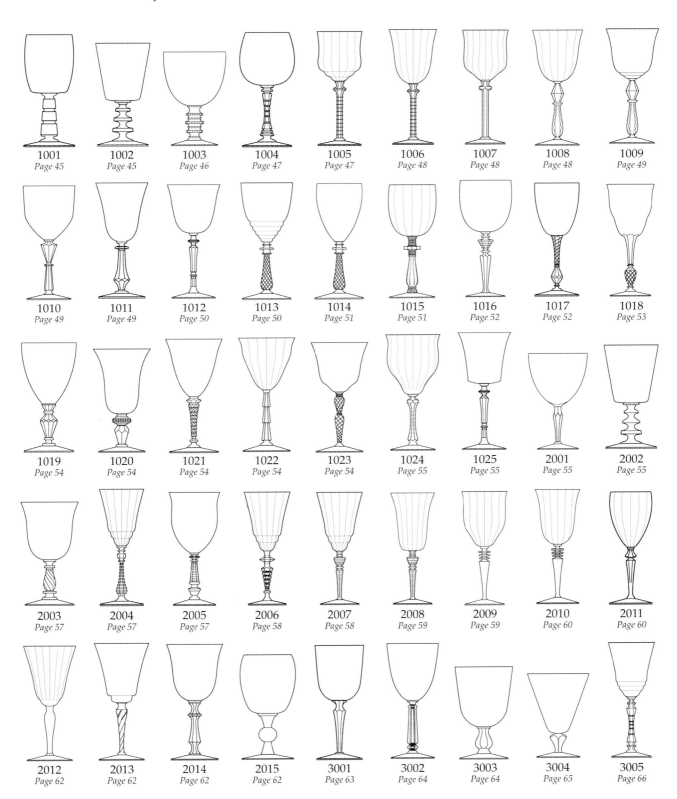

| 1001 | 1002 | 1003 | 1004 | 1005 | 1006 | 1007 | 1008 | 1009 |
| *Page 45* | *Page 45* | *Page 46* | *Page 47* | *Page 47* | *Page 48* | *Page 48* | *Page 48* | *Page 49* |

| 1010 | 1011 | 1012 | 1013 | 1014 | 1015 | 1016 | 1017 | 1018 |
| *Page 49* | *Page 49* | *Page 50* | *Page 50* | *Page 51* | *Page 51* | *Page 52* | *Page 52* | *Page 53* |

| 1019 | 1020 | 1021 | 1022 | 1023 | 1024 | 1025 | 2001 | 2002 |
| *Page 54* | *Page 54* | *Page 54* | *Page 54* | *Page 54* | *Page 55* | *Page 55* | *Page 55* | *Page 55* |

| 2003 | 2004 | 2005 | 2006 | 2007 | 2008 | 2009 | 2010 | 2011 |
| *Page 57* | *Page 57* | *Page 57* | *Page 58* | *Page 58* | *Page 59* | *Page 59* | *Page 60* | *Page 60* |

| 2012 | 2013 | 2014 | 2015 | 3001 | 3002 | 3003 | 3004 | 3005 |
| *Page 62* | *Page 62* | *Page 62* | *Page 62* | *Page 63* | *Page 64* | *Page 64* | *Page 65* | *Page 66* |

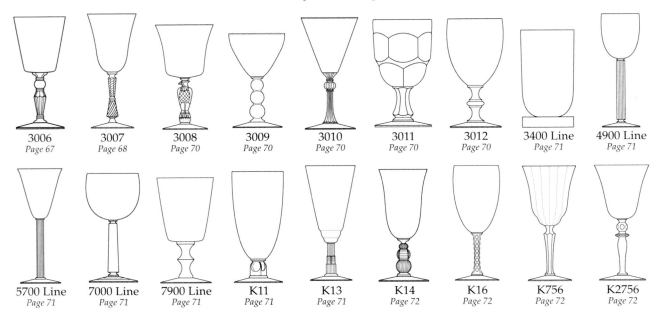

3006	3007	3008	3009	3010	3011	3012	3400 Line	4900 Line
Page 67	*Page 68*	*Page 70*	*Page 70*	*Page 70*	*Page 70*	*Page 70*	*Page 71*	*Page 71*

5700 Line	7000 Line	7900 Line	K11	K13	K14	K16	K756	K2756
Page 71	*Page 71*	*Page 71*	*Page 71*	*Page 71*	*Page 72*	*Page 72*	*Page 72*	*Page 72*

K9058
Page 72

The "7900 Line" and the "1818 Line" are represented by the same illustration. The "1818 Line" was machine made glassware, whereas the "7900 Line" was mouth blown.

Libbey/Rock Sharpe

This early nineteenth-century etching illustrates the New England Glass Company's prosperous beginnings.

Libbey/Rock Sharpe
Stems by Pattern & Number

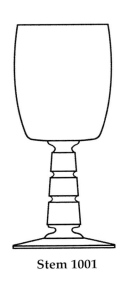

Stem 1001

Apollo
Cut
1001

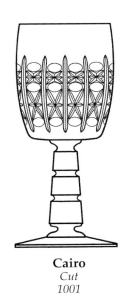

Cairo
Cut
1001

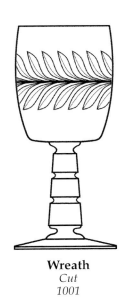

Wreath
Cut
1001

1001-1
Cut
1001

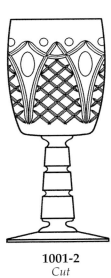

1001-2
Cut
1001

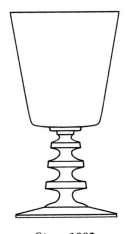

Stem 1002
3 Discs

Corral
Cut
1002

Galway
Cut
1002

Leaf in Arch
Cut
1002

Montclair
Cut
1002

Nassau
Cut
1002

Pickett
Cut
1002

Ridgeway
Cut
1002

Rugby
Cut
1002

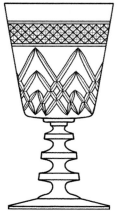

Shannon
Cut
1002

Sheraton
Cut
1002

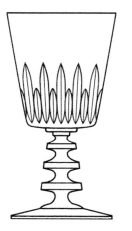

Spike
Cut
1002

Washington
Cut
1002

Westminster
Cut
1002

1002-1
Cut
1002

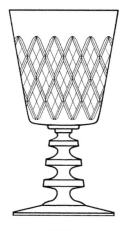

1002-4
Cut
1002

1002-5
Cut
1002

1002-6
Cut
1002

1002-7
Cut
1002

1002-8
Cut
1002

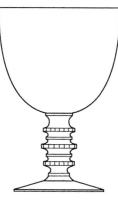

Stem 1003

Bunker Hill
Cut
1003

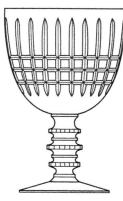

Madison
Cut
1003

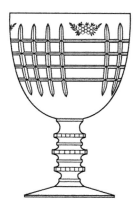

Puritan
Cut
1003

Saratoga
Cut
1003

Stem 1004

Alpine
Cut
1004

Atlantis
Cut, aka "Rosecranz"
1004

Baden
Cut
1004

Villars
Cut
1004

1004-1
Cut
1004

1004-2
Cut
1004

Stem 1005

Burleigh
Cut
1005

Dawn
Cut
1005

Del Mar
Cut
1005

Elaine
Cut
1005

Romance
Cut
1005

1005-1
Cut
1005

1005-2
Cut
1005

1005-3
Cut
1005

Stem 1006

Baltimore
Cut
1006

Stem 1007

Knickerbocker
Cut
1007

1007-1
Cut
1007

1007-2
Cut
1007

1007-3
Cut
1007

1007-4
Cut
1007

Stem 1008

Buckingham
Cut
1008

Lido
Cut
1008

Marina
Cut
1008

1008-1
Cut
1008

1008-2
Cut
1008

1008-3
Cut
1008

1008-4
Cut
1008

Stem 1009

Embassy
Cut
1009

Stem 1010

Piccadilly
Cut
1010

Royale
Cut
1010

1010-1
Cut
1010

1010-2
Cut
1010

1010-3
Cut
1010

1010-4
Cut
1010

1010-5
Cut
1010

Stem 1011

Charleston
Cut
1011

Hancock
Cut
1011

Old Mirror
Cut
1011

Salem
Cut
1011

Williamsburg
Cut
1011

Wisterhouse
Cut
1011

Stem 1012

Antoinette
Cut
1012

Ardmore
Cut
1012

Chalet
Cut
1012

Fontenay
Cut
1012

Miranda
Cut
1012

Riviera
Cut
1012

1012-1
Cut
1012

Stem 1013

Arvida
Cut
1013

Breton
Cut
1013

Dixie
Cut
1013

Groton
Cut
1013

Oradea
Cut
1013

1013-2
Cut
1013

1013-3
Cut
1013

Stem 1014

Hastings
Cut
1014

Stem 1015

Brittany
Cut
1015

Cairo
Cut
1015

Denbeigh
Cut
1015

Frontenac
Cut
1015

Lady Stuart
Cut
1015

Paisley
Cut
1015

Queen Ann
Cut
1015

Symphony
Cut
1015

1015-1
Cut
1015

1015-2
Cut
1015

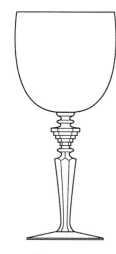

Stem 1016

Countess
Cut
1016

Shasta
Cut
1016

1016-1
Cut
1016

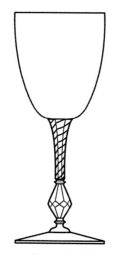

Stem 1017

Burma
Cut
1017

Chantilly
Cut
1017

Cranbrook
Cut
1017

Maritime
Cut
1017

Marlowe
Cut
1017

Persian
Cut
1017

Provincial
Cut
1017

Rhondo
Cut
1017

Rosemary
Cut
1017

Simplicity
Cut
1017

Stardust
Cut
1017

Uxbridge
Cut
1017

1017-1
Cut
1017

Stem 1018

Amesbury
Cut
1018

Bagdad
Cut
1018

Pytonga
Cut
1018

Tempo
Cut
1018

1018-1
Cut
1018

1018-2
Cut
1018

1018-3
Cut
1018

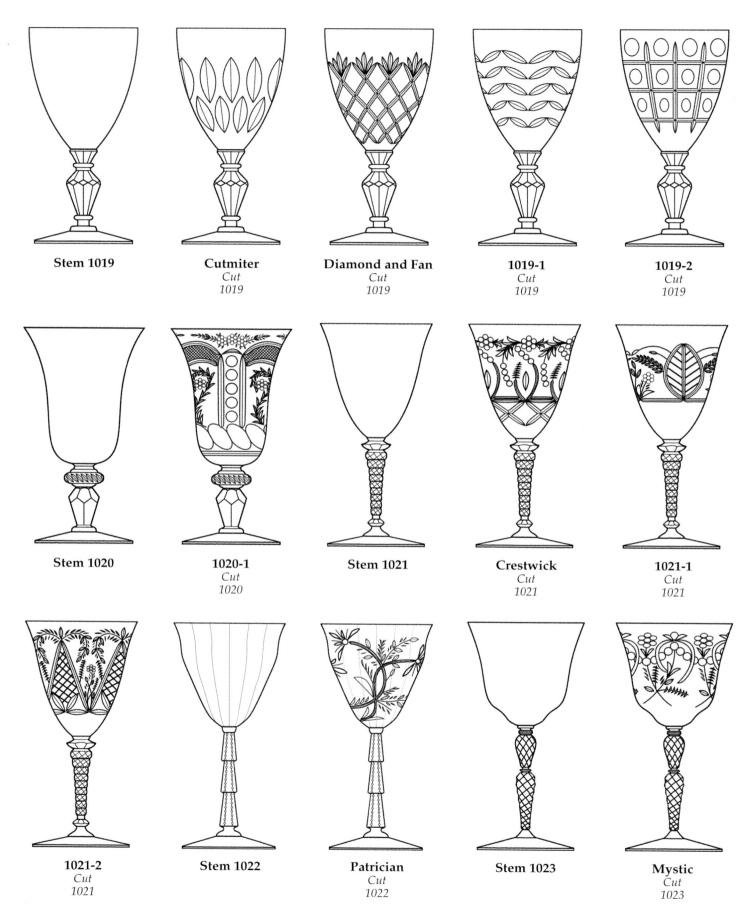

Stem 1019

Cutmiter
Cut
1019

Diamond and Fan
Cut
1019

1019-1
Cut
1019

1019-2
Cut
1019

Stem 1020

1020-1
Cut
1020

Stem 1021

Crestwick
Cut
1021

1021-1
Cut
1021

1021-2
Cut
1021

Stem 1022

Patrician
Cut
1022

Stem 1023

Mystic
Cut
1023

Salon
Cut
1023

1023-1
Cut
1023

Stem 1024

1024-1
Cut
1024

Stem 1025

1025-1
Cut
1025

Stem 2001

Tiara
Cut
2001

Wild Cherry
Cut
2001

2001-1
Cut
2001

Stem 2002
Bowl has a Safety Rim

Aristocrat
Cut
2002

Baguette
Cut
2002

Bramble
Cut
2002

Charm
Cut
2002

Cherie
Cut
2002

Circle and Square
Cut
2002

Coronation
Cut
2002

Empire Wreath
Cut
2002

Fleur de Lis
Cut
2002

Garden Gate
Cut
2002

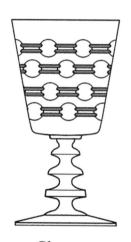

Glasgow
Cut
2002

Gloria
Cut
2002

Heather
Cut
2002

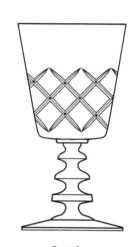

Lattice
Cut
2002

Londonderry
Cut
2002

Olive and Cross
Cut
2002

Radiance
Cut
2002

Rapture
Cut
2002

Ridgewood
Cut
2002

Spear & Ring
Cut
2002

Sultana
Cut
2002

Victoria
Cut
2002

Windover
Cut
2002

Stem 2003

Haddon
Cut
2003

Sutton
Cut
2003

Virginia
Cut
2003

2003-1
Cut
2003

Stem 2004

2004-1
Cut
2004

2004-2
Cut
2004

Stem 2005

Cambria
Cut
2005

Dudley
Cut
2005

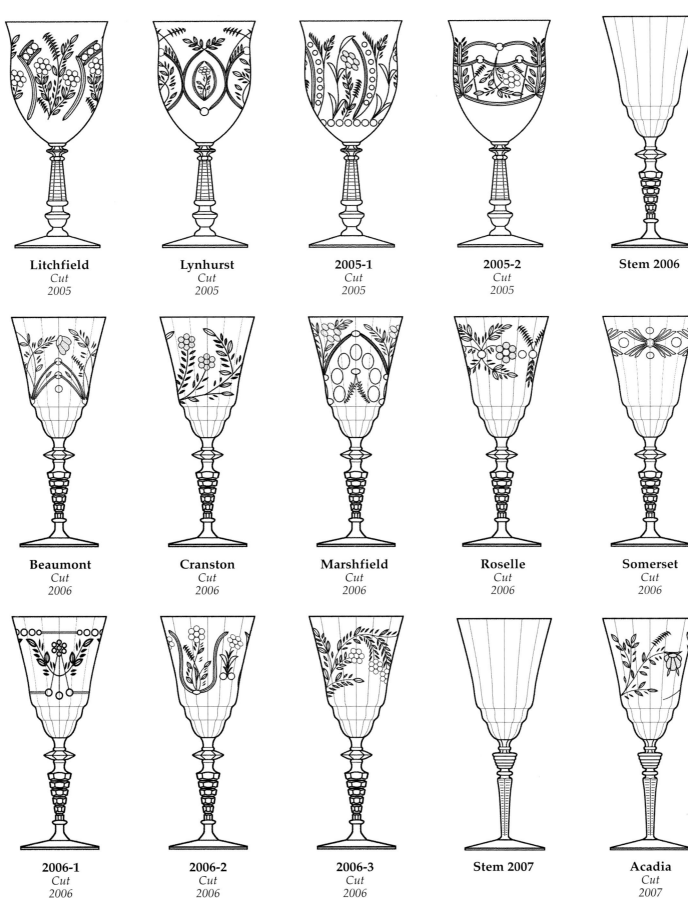

Litchfield
Cut
2005

Lynhurst
Cut
2005

2005-1
Cut
2005

2005-2
Cut
2005

Stem 2006

Beaumont
Cut
2006

Cranston
Cut
2006

Marshfield
Cut
2006

Roselle
Cut
2006

Somerset
Cut
2006

2006-1
Cut
2006

2006-2
Cut
2006

2006-3
Cut
2006

Stem 2007

Acadia
Cut
2007

2007-1
Cut
2007

2007-2
Cut
2007

Stem 2008

Chatham
Cut
2008

Rembrandt
Cut, aka "Claremont"
2008

2008-1
Cut
2008

2008-2
Cut
2008

2008-3
Cut
2008

Stem 2009

Mosque Rose
Cut
2009

Spode
Cut
2009

2009-1
Cut
2009

2009-2
Cut
2009

2009-3
Cut
2009

2009-4
Cut
2009

2009-5
Cut
2009

2009-6
Cut
2009

2009-7
Cut
2009

2009-8
Cut
2009

Stem 2010

Cherokee
Cut
2010

Fernwood
Cut
2010

2010-1
Cut
2010

2010-2
Cut
2010

2010-3
Cut
2010

2010-4
Cut
2010

2010-5
Cut
2010

2010-6
Cut
2010

Stem 2011

Anniversary
Cut
2011

Fuchsia
Cut
2011

Granada
Cut
2011

Wild Rose
Cut
2011

2011-1
Cut
2011

2011-2
Cut
2011

2011-3
Cut
2011

2011-4
Cut
2011

2011-5
Cut
2011

2011-6
Cut
2011

2011-7
Cut
2011

2011-8
Cut
2011

2011-9
Cut
2011

2011-10
Cut
2011

2011-11
Cut
2011

2011-12
Cut
2011

2011-13
Cut
2011

2011-14
Cut
2011

2011-15
Cut
2011

Stem 2012

Buttercup
Cut
2012

Stem 2013

2013-1
Cut
2013

2013-2
Cut
2013

2013-3
Cut
2013

2013-4
Cut
2013

Stem 2014

Marlene
Cut
2014

2014-2
Cut
2014

Stem 2015

2015-1
Cut
2015

2015-2
Cut
2015

Stem 3001
Bowl has a Safety Rim

Candlelight
Cut
3001

Carlton
Cut Balls
3001

Carlton
Cut Flowers
3001

Coronet
Gold
3001

Embassy
Cut
3001

Fernwood
Cut
3001

Glenmore
Cut
3001

Jenny
Cut
3001

Priscilla
Cut
3001

Starlight
Cut
3001

Windswept
Cut
3001

3001-2
Cut
3001

3001-3
Cut
3001

Stem 3002
Bowl has a Safety Rim

Crystal Garland
Cut
3002

Crystal Leaf
Cut
3002

Silver Leaf
Silver and Gray Design
aka "Silver Foliage",3002

3002-1
Cut
3002

3002-2
Cut
3002

3002-3
Cut
3002

3002-4
Cut
3002

Stem 3003
Bowl has a Safety Rim

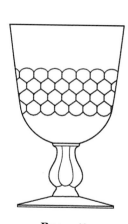

Baguette
Cut
3003

Coin-Cut Classic
Cut
3003

Colonial Heritage
Cut
3003

Diamond Cut
Cut
3003

Fairfax
Cut
3003

Golden Foliage
Gold Design
3003

Laurel Classic
Cut
3003

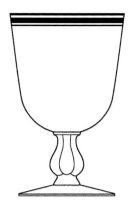

Moonmist
Platinum Bands
3003

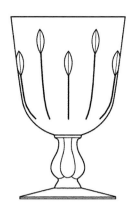

Neptune
Cut
3003

Pastorale
Cut
3003

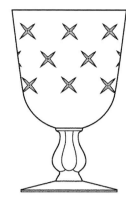

Stardust
Cut, aka "Repose"
3003

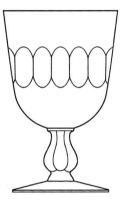

Terrace
Cut
3003

Wheat
Cut
3003

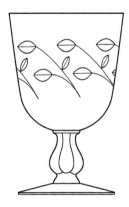

3003-1
Cut
3003

3003-3
Cut
3003

3003-4
Gold and White Design
3003

3003-5
Cut
3003

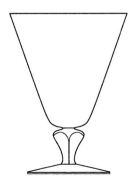

Stem 3004
Bowl has a Safety Rim

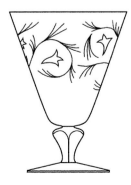

Royal Fern
Gold and White Design
3004

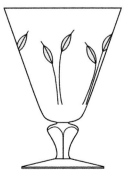

Simplicity
Cut
3004

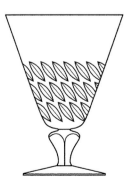

Standish
Cut
3004

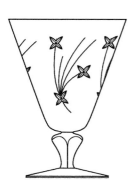

Star Shower
Cut
3004

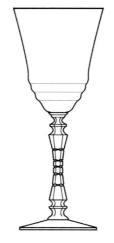

Stem 3005
Bowl has a Safety Rim

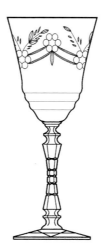

Arctic Rose
Cut, aka "Dover"
3005

Berkley
Cut
3005

Halifax
Cut
3005

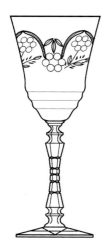

Normandy
Cut, aka "Tropic Rose"
3005

3005-1
Cut
3005

3005-2
Cut
3005

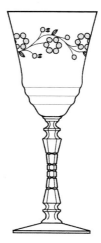

3005-3
Cut
3005

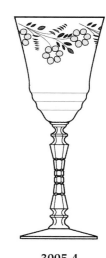

3005-4
Cut
3005

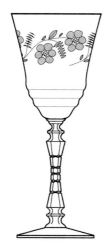

3005-5
Cut
3005

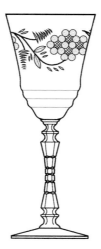

3005-6
Cut
3005

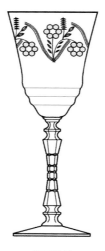

3005-7
Cut
3005

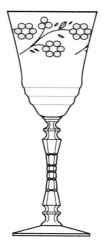

3005-8
Cut
3005

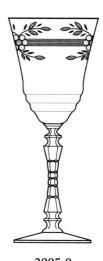

3005-9
Cut
3005

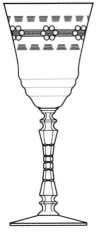

3005-10
Cut
3005

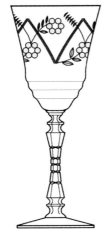

3005-11
Cut
3005

3005-12
Cut
3005

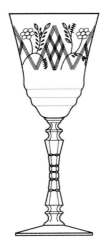

3005-13
Cut
3005

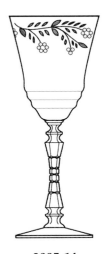

3005-14
Cut
3005

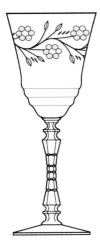

3005-15
Cut
3005

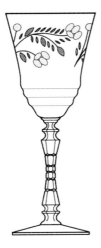

3005-16
Cut
3005

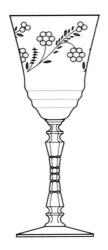

3005-17
Cut
3005

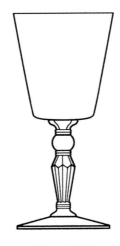

Stem 3006
Bowl has a Safety Rim

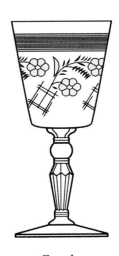

Caprice
Cut
3006

Fern
Cut
3006

Glamour
Cut
3006

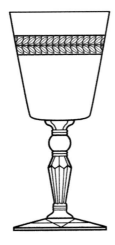

Jefferson
Cut
3006

Luna
Cut
3006

Luxury
Cut
3006

Polished Rain
Cut
3006

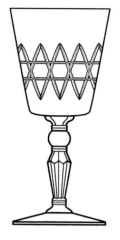

Vanity
Cut
3006

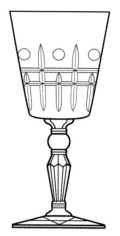

Wayne
Cut
3006

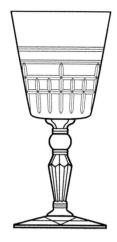

3006-2
Cut
3006

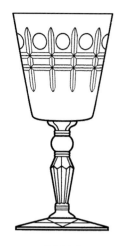

3006-3
Cut
3006

3006-4
Cut
3006

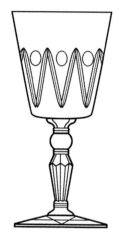

3006-5
Cut
3006

3006-6
Cut
3006

3006-7
Cut
3006

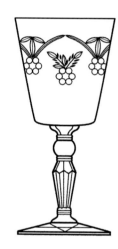

3006-8
Cut
3006

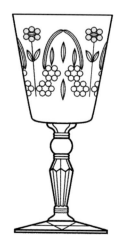

3006-9
Cut
3006

3006-10
Cut
3006

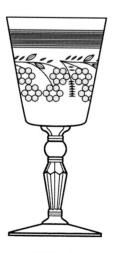

3006-11
Cut
3006

Stem 3007
Bowl has a Safety Rim

Blossoms
Cut
3007

Cameo
Cut
3007

Carol
Cut
3007

Classic
Cut
3007

Colonade
Cut
3007

Corinth
Cut
3007

Dartelle
Cut
3007

Debut
Cut
3007

Eclipse
Cut
3007

Fernleigh
Cut
3007

Formal
Cut
3007

Frond
Cut
3007

Gothic
Cut
3007

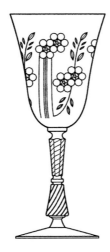

Grecian
Cut
3007

Raindrop
Cut
3007

Rock Garden
Cut
3007

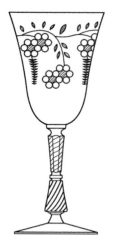

Shah
Cut
3007

Snowberry
Cut
3007

Starlight
Cut
3007

Swirl
Cut
3007

Sylvan
Cut
3007

Teardrop
Cut
3007

3007-6
Cut
3007

Liberty Bell
Bowl has a Safety Rim
3008

Knob Hill
Bowl has a Safety Rim
3009

Stardust
Bowl has a Safety Rim
3010

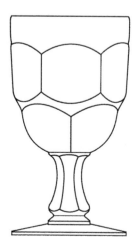

Ashburton
Heavy Pressed Pattern
3011

Stem 3012
Bowl has a Safety Rim

Fern
Cut
3012

Garland
Cut
3012

Peach Bloom
Cut
3012

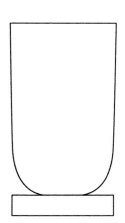

Knickerbocker
Cut, Square Base
3400 Line, Signed
"Libbey"

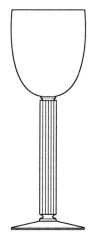

Embassy
Flat, Ribbed Stem
4900 Line, Signed
"Libbey"

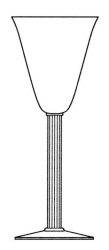

Monticello
Round, Ribbed Stem
5700 Line, Signed
"Libbey"

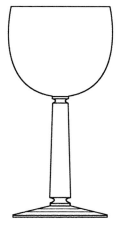

American Prestige
Square, Cut Stem
7000 Line, Signed
"Libbey"

Waterford
7900 Line
Signed "Libbey"

Jamestown
Cut,"1818 Line"
Signed "Libbey"

Raleigh
Cut,"1818 Line"
Signed "Libbey"

Williamsburg
Cut,"1818 Line"
Signed "Libbey"

Yorktown
Cut,"1818 Line"
Signed "Libbey"

Stem K11
Signed "Libbey"

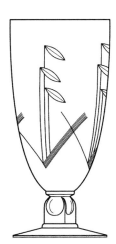

Sonata
Cut, K11-1029
Signed "Libbey"

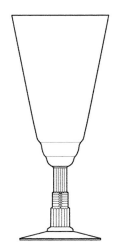

Stem K13
Signed "Libbey"

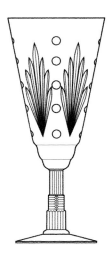

Lucerne
Cut, K13-1039
Signed "Libbey"

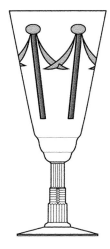

Malmaison
Cut, K13-1034
Signed "Libbey"

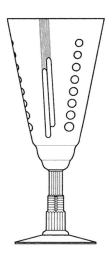

Moonbeam
Cut, K13-1037
Signed "Libbey"

Stem K14
Signed "Libbey"

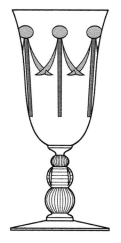

Antoinette
Cut, K14-1034
Signed "Libbey"

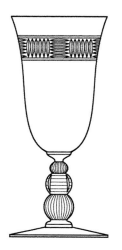

Devonshire
Cut, K14-1036
Signed "Libbey"

Neptune
Cut, K14-1024
Signed "Libbey"

Stem K16
Signed "Libbey"

Waterwitch
Cut, K16-1031
Signed "Libbey"

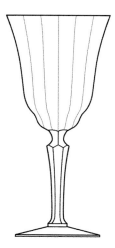

Stem K756
Signed "Libbey"

Kenmore
Cut, K756-062
Signed "Libbey"

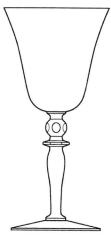

Stem K2756
Signed "Libbey"

Diana
Cut, K2756-08
Signed "Libbey"

Gloria
Cut, K2756-10
Signed "Libbey"

Stem K9058
Signed "Libbey"

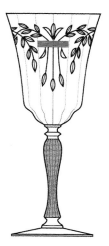

Garland
Cut, K9058-06
Signed "Libbey"

Vesta
Platinum Bands, K9058
Signed "Libbey"

Hawkes

The T.G. Hawkes Company remained in the same structure for the duration of the 82 years it was in businesss.

Hawkes Crystal

The Hawkes Rich Cut Glass Works was established in 1880 in Corning, New York. In 1890, the firm was incorporated as T. G. Hawkes & Co. In its day, the Hawkes Company epitomized the finest in cut glass production, creating over 300 outstandingly beautiful cut and engraved stemware patterns and other pieces. The company was exclusively a decorating outlet and purchased all of its blanks (undecorated glass) from outside sources.

The Hawkes Tiffin Company was founded by Thomas Gibbons Hawkes, who migrated here from Ireland at age 17. Thomas had studied civil engineering in school, but ended up in the glass business perhaps due to the pull of his ancestral ties.

He descended from two families with generations of experience in the glass world: the Hawkes family of Dudley, England, and the Penrose family of Waterford, Ireland. The Penrose name was linked to the founding of Waterford Glass. Thomas Hawkes of Dudley was reportedly the first person in England to make deeply cut glass. Prior to founding the Hawkes Company, Thomas was employed ten years as a foreman at the glass cutting firm of Hoare & Dailey in Corning.

When Thomas Hawkes died in 1913, his son, Samuel, who was already apprenticed in the glass trade, became President of the Hawkes Company, operating it successfully for thirty years. The company would remain a family-run enterprise until its closing in 1962.

During its 82 years in business, T. G. Hawkes & Company captured world-wide attention for its products, designing crystal services for members of royalty and at least two U.S. Presidents. Designs were masterfully executed on dozens or shapes and weights of glass. Customers could choose from a large variety of bowl shapes and stem forms and choice of a round or square foot. For many years, Hawkes also ran a replacement service for their active and discontinued patterns.

Hawkes' large array of stemware, so highly prized today, often came with magnificent serving pieces, such as compotes, cruets, mayonnaise sets, and punch bowls. Enormous amounts of bar ware and bar accessories were produced, including decanters, martini pitchers, bitters bottles and ice buckets. Many home accent items were also made - picture frames, lamps and vases - as well as lovely cologne and perfume bottles. Hawkes' products were sold at leading jewelry stores and major department stores in the United States, Canada, and overseas.

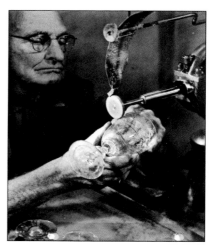

The firm's logo was a trefoil form enclosing a hawk in each of the two bottom lobes with a fleur-de-lis in the center. By 1920, only the acid-etched name HAWKES began to appear. About half the pieces are marked.

During the early years of operation, the Hawkes Company obtained the majority of its blanks from the

Above Photo: Copper-engraving on "blank" 7330.
Below: Polishing the cutting to a smooth brilliance.

74

Hawkes

Steuben Glass Works, a Corning firm that Thomas Hawkes, Frederick Carder and others founded in 1903. Steuben was established mainly to make blanks for Hawkes, however, art glass, similar to the quality of Tiffany's, was also made there. When the Steuben Glass Works was sold to Corning Glass Works in the 20s, Hawkes continued to purchase most of its colored blanks from the Steuben Division of Corning Glass.

Over the years, some of the companies Hawkes obtained blanks from included Duncan and Miller, Dorflinger and Sons, Tiffin Glass, A. H. Heisey, Libbey Glass, Seneca Glass, and Thomas Webb and Sons of England. The quality of many of the manufacturers' blanks varied, depending on the orders set forth by Hawkes. Occasionally, in Hawkes' catalogues, the blank producer is mentioned.

The Hawkes Company's early decorating techniques mainly emphasized cutting and engraving. Both colored blanks and blanks with applied color were decorated at the firm. Cut designs usually bore geometric motifs, however some floral decorations were also produced. Engraving designs included enchanting pictorial scenes, animals and flowers.

Hawkes offered various styles of engraving, including relief (the design is raised above the background) and intaglio (the design is cut below the surface). Hawkes' intaglio glass carried a separate trademark and was known as Gravic Glass. Enameling, silvering, and gilding were some of the other decorating methods used by Hawkes in later years.

T. G. Hawkes & Company enjoyed great prosperity for almost the first half of the century. After World War II, however, after Samuel Hawkes retired, the company began to record financial losses. Thomas Hawkes' nephew, Penrose Hawkes, took control of the firm, but his efforts would be to no avail. The company racked up substantial losses in the 50's and in 1962 a decision was made to cease operations.

The Tiffin Glass Company of Tiffin, Ohio, purchased Hawkes' trademarks, patterns and equipment in 1964 with the intention of establishing the T. G. Hawkes Division of Tiffin. While Tiffin Glass did produce some Hawkes patterns, the Hawkes line was never developed as originally envisioned.

In 1984, Jim Maxwell, a former Tiffin Glass cutter, bought the Tiffin molds and equipment. Eight years later, he began producing four Hawkes patterns under Maxwell Crystal, Inc. The company is still in business, located in Tiffin, Ohio.

A roughing technique was used to create the basic cut pattern design on Hawkes Crystal.

Hawkes at one time offered over 322 different cutting and engraving patterns. Employees are shown here smoothing from the line-shaft.

Hawkes
Stems by Shape & Number

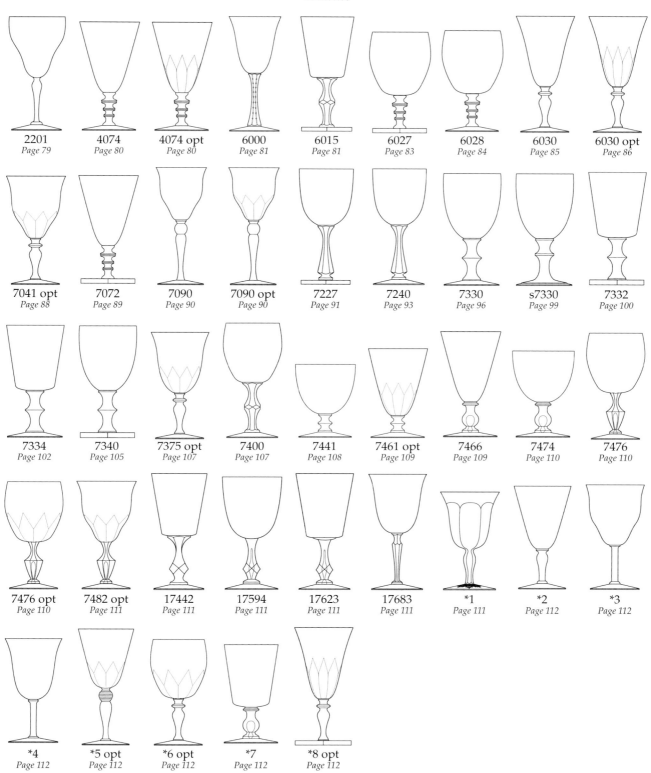

2201
Page 79

4074
Page 80

4074 opt
Page 80

6000
Page 81

6015
Page 81

6027
Page 83

6028
Page 84

6030
Page 85

6030 opt
Page 86

7041 opt
Page 88

7072
Page 89

7090
Page 90

7090 opt
Page 90

7227
Page 91

7240
Page 93

7330
Page 96

s7330
Page 99

7332
Page 100

7334
Page 102

7340
Page 105

7375 opt
Page 107

7400
Page 107

7441
Page 108

7461 opt
Page 109

7466
Page 109

7474
Page 110

7476
Page 110

7476 opt
Page 110

7482 opt
Page 111

17442
Page 111

17594
Page 111

17623
Page 111

17683
Page 111

*1
Page 111

*2
Page 112

*3
Page 112

*4
Page 112

*5 opt
Page 112

*6 opt
Page 112

*7
Page 112

*8 opt
Page 112

*Stem #'s 1-8 are not Hawkes factory assigned numbers, but were assigned by the authors for reference purposes.

Hawkes
Stems by Pattern & Number

Stem 2201

Aquila
Cut
2201

Avalon
Cut
2201

Clarendon
Cut
2201

Delhi
Cut
2201

Essex
Cut
2201

Fern
Cut
2201

Fruits Border
Cut
2201

Henley
Cut
2201

"L"
Cut, Also Satin "L"
2201

Laurel
Cut
2201

Marcella
Cut, Also Satin Marcella
2201

Satin Louise
Cut, Gray
2201

Wheat
Also Satin Wheat
2201

2201-1
Gray Engraving
2201

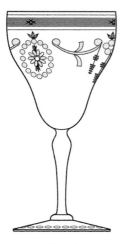

2201-2
Gray Engraving
2201

Stem 4074

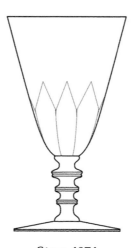

Stem 4074
Optic

Delft Diamond
Cut
4074

Donisel
Cut
4074

Dudley
Cut
4074

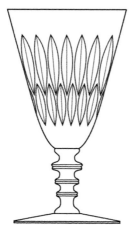

Eardley
Cut
4074

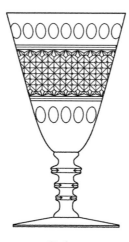

Foley
Cut
4074

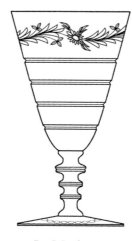

Le Moderne
Cut
4074

Munster
Cut
4074

Mystic
Cut
4074

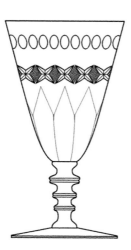

Savoy
Cut
4074

Vernay
Cut
4074

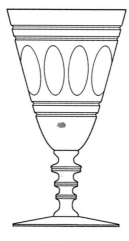

Walpole
Cut
4074

Wexford
Cut
4074

4074-1
Cut
4074

Stem 6000

Aster
Cut
6000

Clarendon
Cut
6000

Coronet
Cut
6000

Empire
Cut
6000

Francis I
Cut
6000

Majestic
Cut
6000

Talisman
Cut
6000

Victoria
Cut
6000

6000-1
Cut
6000

Stem 6015
Square Base

Birr
Cut
6015

Carnation
Cut
6015

China Aster
Cut
6015

Dagney
Cut
6015

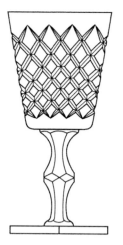

Delft Diamond
Cut
6015

Donisel #2
Cut
6015

Downing
Cut
6015

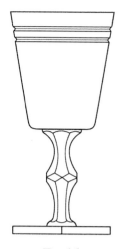

Druid
Cut
6015

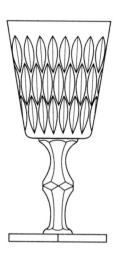

Eardley
Cut
6015

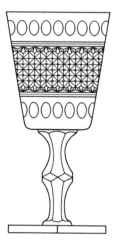

Foley
Cut
6015

Gravic Fruits
Cut
6015

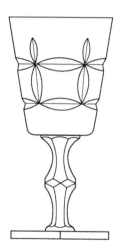

Kerry
Cut
6015

Kings
Cut
6015

Kohinoor
Cut
6015

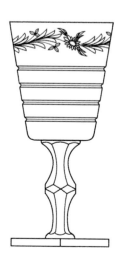

Le Moderne
Cut
6015

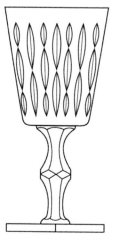

Mallory
Cut
6015

Marquis of Waterford
Cut
6015

Mitres & Fruits
Cut
6015

Munster
Cut
6015

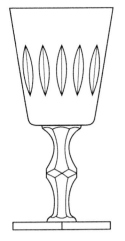

Ramsey
Cut
6015

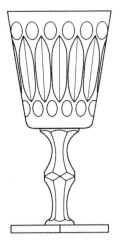

Regal
Cut
6015

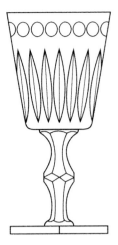

St. George
Cut
6015

Satin Iris
Cut
6015

Strawberry, Diamond & Fan
Cut
6015

Thousand Eyes
Cut
6015

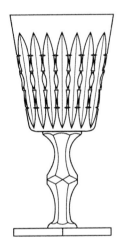

Triumph
Cut
6015

Twist & Fruits
Cut
6015

Vernay
Cut
6015

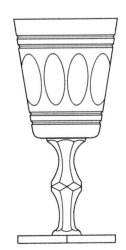

Walpole
Cut
6015

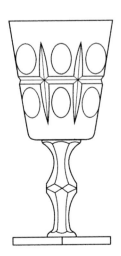

Wexford
Cut
6015

Wild Rose
Cut
6015

Stem 6027
Square Base

Dagney
Cut
6027

Delft Diamond
Cut
6027

Donisel
Cut
6027

Downing
Cut
6027

Dudley
Cut
6027

Foley
Cut
6027

Manor
Cut
6027

Monarch
Cut
6027

Munster
Cut
6027

St. George
Cut
6027

Strawberry, Diamond & Fan
Cut
6027

Thousand Eyes
Cut
6027

Token
Cut
6027

York
Cut
6027

6027-1
Cut
6027

Stem 6028

Cranford
Cut
6028

Delft Diamond
Cut
6028

Donisel
Cut
6028

Downing
Cut
6028

Dudley
Cut
6028

Manor
Cut
6028

Monarch
Cut
6028

Munster
Cut
6028

Mystic
Cut
6028

St. George
Cut
6028

Strawberry, Diamond & Fan
Cut
6028

Thousand Eyes
Cut
6028

Token
Cut
6028

York
Cut
6028

Stem 6030

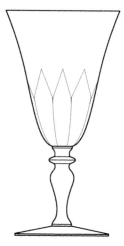

Stem 6030
Optic

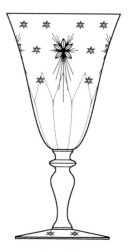

Aquila
Cut
6030

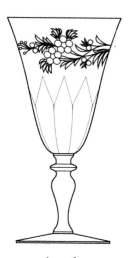

Argyle
Cut
6030

Avalon
Cut
6030

Barstow
Cut
6030

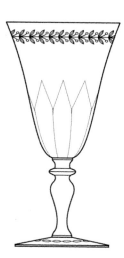

Bellwood
Cut
6030

Chantilly
Cut
6030

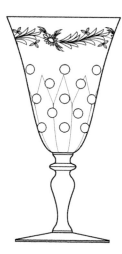

Christina
Cut
6030

Coronet
Cut
6030

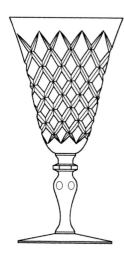

Delft Diamond
Cut
6030

Diana
Cut, aka Cleo
6030

Donisel
Cut
6030

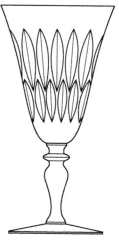

Eardley
Cut
6030

Gravic Fruits
Cut
6030

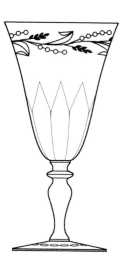

Henley
Cut
6030

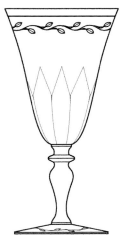

"L"
Cut
6030

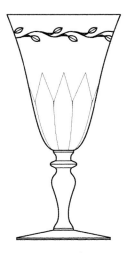

Laurel
Cut, Also Satin Laurel
6030

Mitres & Fruits
Cut
6030

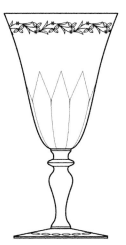

Patricia
Cut
6030

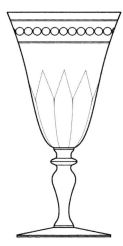

Pearl Border
Cut
6030

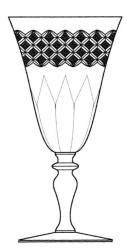

Pierre
Cut
6030

Ramsey
Cut
6030

Rye
Cut
6030

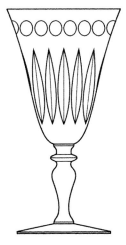

St. George
Cut
6030

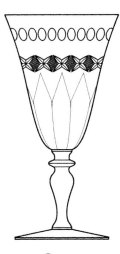

Savoy
Cut
6030

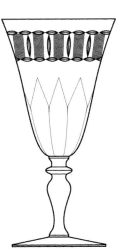

Sheraton Border
Cut
6030

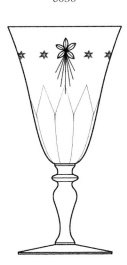

Starlight
Cut
6030

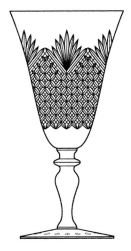

Strawberry, Diamond & Fan
Cut
6030

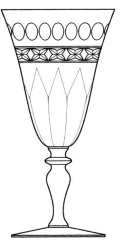

Valeria
Cut
6030

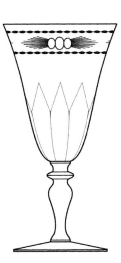

Warwick Border
Cut
6030

Wexford
Cut
6030

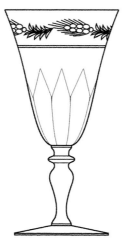

Wheat Border
Also Satin Wheat Border
6030

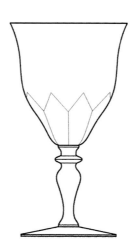

Stem 7041
Optic

Beverly
Cut
7041

Calais
Cut
7041

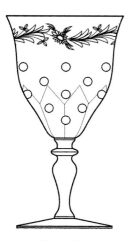

Christina
Cut
7041

Dawn
Cut
7041

Diana
Cut, aka Cleo
7041

Francis I
Cut
7041

Francis I
"Special", Cut
7041

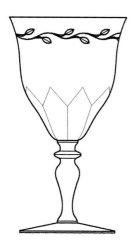

Laurel
Cut, Also Satin Laurel
7041

Louise
Cut
7041

Navarre
Cut
7041

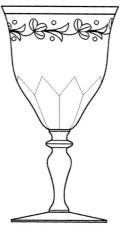

Sylvia
Cut
7041

Victoria
Cut
7041

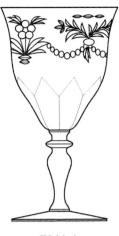

7041-1
Cut
7041

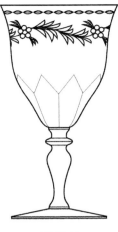

7041-2
Cut
7041

Stem 7072
Square Base

Carnation
Cut
7072

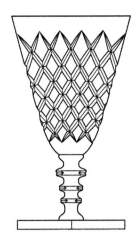

Delft Diamond
Cut
7072

Donisel
Cut
7072

Dudley
Cut
7072

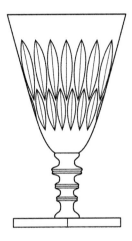

Eardley
Cut
7072

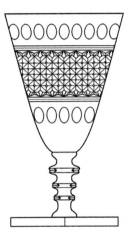

Foley
Cut
7072

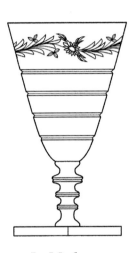

Le Moderne
Cut
7072

Mitres & Fruits
Cut
7072

Mystic
Cut
7072

St. George
Cut
7072

Vernay
Cut
7072

Walpole
Cut
7072

Wexford
Cut
7072

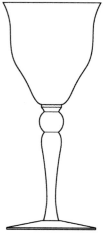

Stem 7090

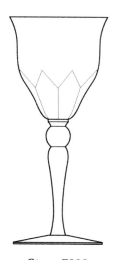

Stem 7090
Optic

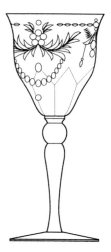

Avalon
Cut
7090

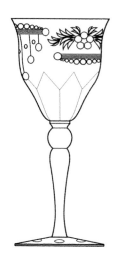

Beverly
Cut
7090

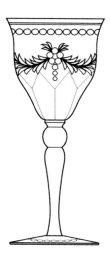

Calais
Cut
7090

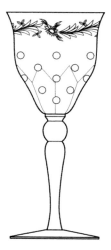

Christina
Cut
7090

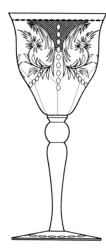

Clarendon
Cut
7090

Coronet
Cut
7090

Francis I
Cut
7090

Francis I
"Special", Cut
7090

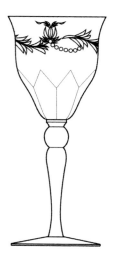

Louise
Cut
7090

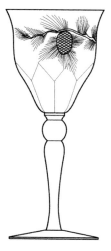

Pine
Cut
7090

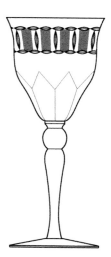

Sheraton Border
Cut
7090

Victoria
Cut
7090

7090-1
Cut
7090

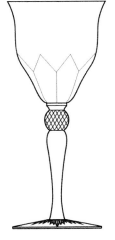

7090-2
Cut
7090

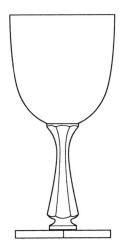

Stem 7227
Square Base

Barcroft
Cut
7227

Carnation
Cut
7227

China Aster
Cut
7227

Colfax
Cut
7227

Dagney
Cut
7227

Delft Diamond
Cut
7227

Downing
Cut
7227

Druid
Cut
7227

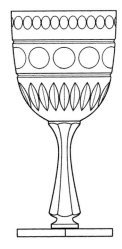

Dudley
Cut
7227

Dunmore
Cut
7227

Eardley
Cut
7227

Gravic Fruits
Cut
7227

Kerry
Cut
7227

Kings
Cut
7227

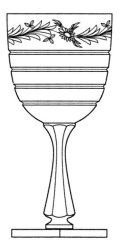

Le Moderne
Cut
7227

Mallory
Cut
7227

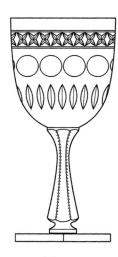

Manor
Cut
7227

Mitres & Fruits
Cut
7227

Monarch
Cut
7227

Mystic
Cut
7227

Parnell
Cut
7227

Regal
Cut
7227

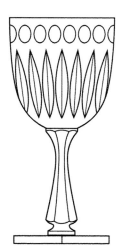

St. George
Cut
7227

Satin Iris
Cut
7227

Sharon
Cut
7227

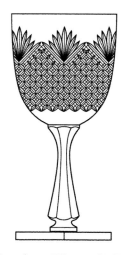

Strawberry, Diamond & Fan
Cut
7227

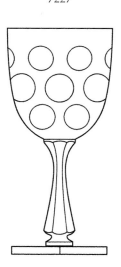

Thousand Eyes
Cut
7227

Token
Cut
7227

Triumph
Cut
7227

Twist
Cut
7227

Vernay
Cut
7227

Wild Rose
Cut
7227

Woodmere
Cut
7227

York
Cut
7227

Stem 7240

Barcroft
Cut
7240

Carnation
Cut
7240

Chelsea Rose
Cut
7240

China Aster
Cut
7240

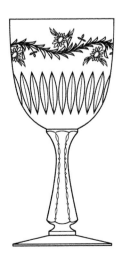

Colfax
Cut
7240

Dagney
Cut
7240

Delft Diamond
Cut
7240

Donisel
Cut
7240

Downing
Cut
7240

Druid
Cut
7240

Eardley
Cut
7240

Fruits Border
Cut
7240

Kerry
Cut
7240

Kings
Cut
7240

La Salle
Cut
7240

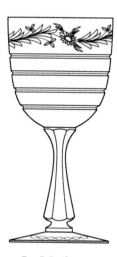

Le Moderne
Cut
7240

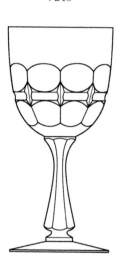

Madison
Cut
7240

Mallory
Cut
7240

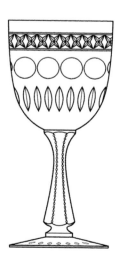

Manor
Cut
7240

Marion
Cut
7240

Mitres & Fruits
Cut
7240

Monarch
Cut
7240

Munster
Cut
7240

Mystic
Cut
7240

Parnell
Cut
7240

Primrose
Cut
7240

Queen's
Cut
7240

Regal
Cut
7240

St. George
Cut
7240

Satin Iris
Cut
7240

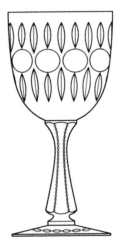

Sierra
Cut
7240

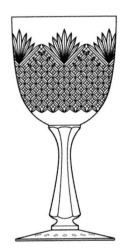

Strawberry, Diamond & Fan
Cut
7240

Talisman
Cut
7240

Thousand Eyes
Cut
7240

Token
Cut
7240

Triumph
Cut
7240

Twist
Cut
7240

Twist & Fruits
Cut
7240

Vernay
Cut
7240

Wild Rose
Cut
7240

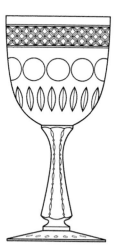

Woodmere
Cut
7240

York
Cut
7240

Stem 7330

Aquila
Cut
7330

Barclay
Also Satin Barclay
7330

Bellwood
Cut
7330

Betty Border
Cut
7330

Carnation
Cut
7330

Chilton
Cut
7330

Colfax
Cut
7330

Colony
Cut
7330

Cornwall
Cut
7330

Dagney
Cut
7330

Dawn
Cut
7330

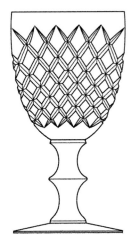

Delft Diamond
Cut
7330

Druid
Cut
7330

Dunmore
Cut
7330

Eardley
Cut
7330

Francis I
Cut
7330

Fruits Border
Also Satin Fruits Border
7330

Jubilee
Cut
7330

Kerry
Cut
7330

Killarney
Cut
7330

Kings
Cut
7330

"L"
Cut
7330

Lady Alice
Cut
7330

Madeira
Cut
7330

Mallory
Cut
7330

Marcella
Cut
7330

Montclair Border
Cut
7330

Mystic
Cut
7330

Pussy Willow
Cut
7330

Regal
Cut
7330

Regent
Cut
7330

Revere
Cut
7330

St. George
Cut
7330

Satin Iris
Cut
7330

Strawberry, Diamond & Fan
Cut
7330

Surrey
Cut
7330

Talisman
Cut
7330

Tally Ho
Cut
7330

Thames
Cut
7330

Twist
Cut
7330

Twist & Fruits
Cut
7330

Vernay
Cut
7330

Victoria
Cut
7330

Wheat
Cut, Also Satin Wheat
7330

Wickham
Cut
7330

Wild Rose
Cut
7330

7330-1
Cut
7330

7330-2
Cut
7330

Stem s7330
Sterling Base

Barclay
Cut
s7330

Betty Border
Cut
s7330

Chilton
Cut
s7330

Colfax
Cut
s7330

Cornwall
Cut
s7330

Francis I
Cut
s7330

Fruits Border
Cut
s7330

Madeira
Cut
s7330

Marcella
Cut
s7330

Strawberry, Diamond & Fan
Cut
s7330

Stem 7332
Square Base

Barcroft
Cut
7332

Birr
Cut
7332

Carnation
Cut
7332

Carthage
Cut
7332

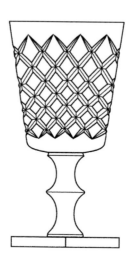

Chilton
Cut
7332

China Aster
Cut
7332

Dagney
Cut
7332

Delft Diamond
Cut
7332

Donisel
Cut
7332

Donisel #2
Cut
7332

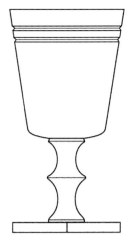

Druid
Cut
7332

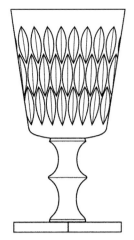

Eardley
Cut
7332

Gravic Fruits
Cut
7332

Kerry
Cut
7332

Kings
Cut
7332

Lady Alice
Cut
7332

Mallory
Cut
7332

Montclair & Fruits Border
Cut
7332

Montclair Border
Cut
7332

Regal
Cut
7332

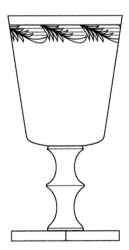

Royal
Cut
7332

St. George
Cut
7332

Satin Iris
Cut
7332

Strawberry, Diamond & Fan
Cut
7332

Tally Ho
Cut
7332

Thames
Cut
7332

Thousand Eyes
Cut
7332

Toltic
Cut
7332

Twist & Fruits
Cut
7332

Vernay
Cut
7332

Wild Rose
Cut
7332

York
Cut
7332

Stem 7334

Barclay
Cut
7334

Barcroft
Cut
7334

Bellwood
Cut
7334

Birr
Cut
7334

Blarney
Cut
7334

Carnation
Cut
7334

Carthage
Cut
7334

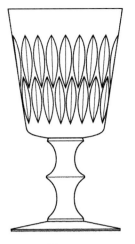

Caven
Cut
7334

Chelsea Rose
Also Satin Chelsea Rose
7334

Clarendon
Cut
7334

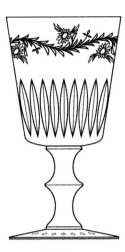

Colfax
Cut
7334

Cornwall
Cut
7334

Dagney
Cut
7334

Dawn
Cut
7334

Delft Diamond
Cut
7334

Donisel #2
Cut
7334

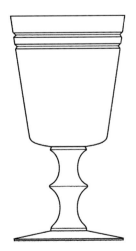

Druid
Cut
7334

Dunmore
Cut
7334

Eardley
Cut
7334

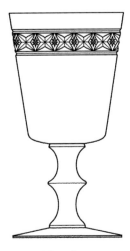

Heather
Cut
7334

Kerry
Cut
7334

Kings
Cut
7334

Kohinoor
Cut
7334

Lady Alice
Cut
7334

Madison
Cut
7334

Mallory
Cut
7334

Marcella
Cut
7334

Monarch
Cut
7334

Montclair Border
Cut
7334

Montclair & Fruits Border
Cut
7334

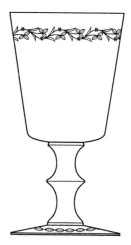

Patricia
Also Satin Patricia
7334

Ramsey
Cut
7334

Regal
Cut
7334

Royal
Cut, Also Satin Royal
7334

Rye
Cut
7334

Satin Iris
Cut
7334

Satin Wheat
Cut
7334

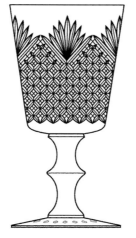

Strawberry, Diamond & Fan
Cut
7334

Sultana
Cut
7334

Tally Ho
Cut
7334

Thames
Cut
7334

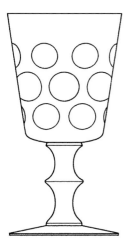

Thousand Eyes
Cut
7334

Twist & Fruits
Cut
7334

Valeria
Cut
7334

Vernay
Cut
7334

Wild Rose
Cut
7334

Woodmere
Cut
7334

Stem 7340
Square Base

Carnation
Cut
7340

Chilton
Cut
7340

Colony
Cut
7340

Cornwall
Cut
7340

Dagney
Cut
7340

Delft Diamond
Cut
7340

Eardley
Cut
7340

Kerry
Cut
7340

Killarney
Cut
7340

Kings
Cut
7340

Mallory
Cut
7340

Mystic
Cut
7340

Regal
Cut
7340

Revere
Cut
7340

Strawberry, Diamond & Fan
Cut
7340

Twist
Cut
7340

Twist & Fruits
Cut
7340

Vernay
Cut
7340

Wickham
Cut
7340

Wild Rose
Cut
7340

Stem 7375
Optic

Allegro
Cut Foot
7375

Laurel
Cut, Also Satin Laurel
7375

Leona
Cut
7375

Louise
Cut
7375

Madeira
Cut
7375

Marcella
Cut
7375

Melody Band
Cut
7375

Pine
Cut
7375

Worcester Rose
Cut, Gray
7375

7375-1
Cut
7375

Stem 7400

Barcroft
Cut
7400

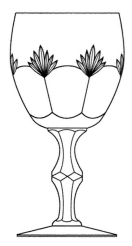

Baron
Cut
7400

Carnation
Cut
7400

Chilton
Cut
7400

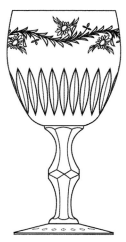

Colfax
Cut
7400

Delft Diamond
Cut
7400

Donisel
Cut
7400

Mallory
Cut
7400

Sierra
Cut
7400

Strawberry, Diamond & Fan
Cut
7400

Vernay
Cut
7400

Wickham
Cut
7400

Stem 7441

Aquila
Cut
7441

Imperial
Cut
7441

Kings
Cut
7441

Satin Wheat
Cut
7441

Strawberry, Diamond & Fan
Cut
7441

Valeria
Cut
7441

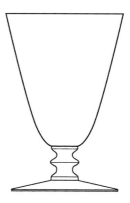

Stem 7461

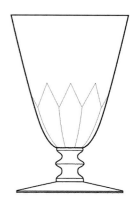

Stem 7461
Optic

Aquila
Cut
7461

Carthage
Cut
7461

Kings
Cut
7461

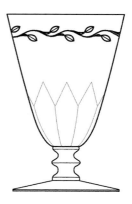

Laurel
Cut
7461

Louise
Cut
7461

Marcella
Cut
7461

Montclair Border
Cut
7461

Valeria
Cut
7461

Worcester Rose
Cut, Gray
7461

Stem 7466

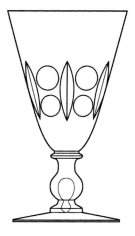

Belfast
Cut
7466

Imperial
Cut
7466

Laurel
Also Satin Laurel
7466

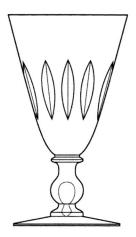

Ramsey
Cut
7466

Ramsey & Caprice
Also Ramsey & Satin Caprice
7466

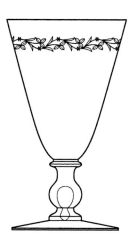

Satin Patricia
Cut
7466

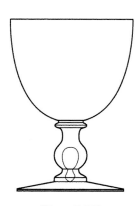

Stem 7474

Imperial
Cut
7474

Othello
Cut
7474

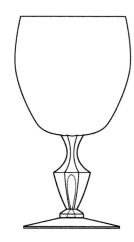

Stem 7476

Stem 7476
Optic

Celeste
Cut
7476

Patricia
Also Satin Patricia
7476

Ramsey
Cut
7476

Starlight
Cut
7476

Strawberry, Diamond & Fan
Cut
7476

Stem 7482
Optic

Laurel
Cut
7482

Modern Border
Cut
7482

Stem 17442

Kilkenny
Cut
17442

Stem 17594

Hermitage
Cut
17594

Stem 17623

Connemara
Cut
17623

Stem 17683

La Scala
Cut, Gold
17683

Richelieu
Cut
17683

Tullaroan
Cut
17683

Colonial
Cut
1

Stem #'s 1-8 are not Hawkes factory assigned numbers, but were assigned by
the authors for reference purposes.

Stem 2

Stem 3

3-1
Gold Bands
3

3-2
Engraved
3

3-3
Engraved
3

Stem 4

4-1
Engraved
3

Stem 5

Stem 6

6-1
Cut
6

Stem 7

Stem 8
Optic
Square Base

Sheraton Border
Cut
8

Stem #'s 1-8 are not Hawkes factory assigned numbers, but were assigned by the authors for reference purposes.

Note: Entries that read "Also Satin ...." mean that the same pattern was made in a gray cutting.

Glastonbury/Lotus
Index by Pattern Name

Definitions:
C - Cut
D - Decoration
E - Etched
GD - Gold Decoration
GE - Gold Encrusted

Libbey/Rock Sharpe
Index by Pattern Name

Hawkes
Index by Pattern Name

Replacements, Ltd.

One thing's for sure: Bob Page has found his calling as founder and owner of Replacements, Ltd. In 1981, Page founded the company which is now the world's largest supplier of obsolete, inactive and active china, crystal and flatware. Replacements grossed $32 million in sales in 1994 and has projected sales of $40 million for 1995. While success has been inspiring for Page, he's not ready to sit back and take it easy. "I love what I do. Every day when I get up I can't wait to get in here, it's really a labor of love" says a youthful-looking, 49-year old Page, who typically puts in 80 hours a week.

Normally, Page goes to work clad in blue jeans and a navy blue T-shirt bearing the Replacements, Ltd. logo. The casual clothing reflects his overall lifestyle, which could be described as low-key for a man in his position. There are no high-priced cars, boats or other obvious signs of wealth as he still lives in a house he bought over twelve years ago.

"To me, the real thrill is in the search. That's what keeps me going," says Page. That search entails locating and stocking tableware for more than 900,000 customers. Most are homemakers seeking to replace or add to their wedding china or everyday pattern. Although there are some celebrities present on Replacements' mailing list: Sally Jessy Raphael orders tableware for her bed and breakfasts; Barbara Walters has purchased Minton china; and Charlton Heston recently ordered several thousand dollars' worth of china for a special dinner.

The company currently maintains over two million pieces of inventory in 56,000 different patterns and is constantly adding to those numbers. To obtain merchandise, Replacements relies on: a network of 3,000 independent suppliers, mostly antique dealers, who canvass flea markets, estate sales and auctions looking for dinnerware in mint condition to sell to the company; china, crystal and flatware manufacturers throughout the world; thousands of individuals who wish to sell their patterns; and its own buyers who spend months on the road buying pieces and sets for the company.

The network of dealers embarks on their search efforts armed with Replacements' Suppliers Index. This 700-page book is published quarterly by the company and contains patterns which Replacements has requests for, as well as the prices it will pay suppliers for merchandise.

One of Replacements' most prolific suppliers is Page himself. When he embarks on a buying trip he never fails to return without a van full of merchandise. "It's really a thrill to find a pattern that I know we have hundreds of requests for," says Page.

Page is especially savvy at finding old crystal by Heisey, Cambridge, Fostoria, Tiffin and others, or finding unusual pieces to display in The Museum at Replacements, Ltd. for Tableware and Decorative Arts, which is located on the premises of the company. One of Page's more interesting buying trips occurred when he flew to Malta and purchased inventory from a store that had been in business since 1902 but had never had a sale.

In it's 225,000-square-foot facility, Replacements has an 8,000-square-foot showroom and nearly $70 million worth of retail inventory.

Replacements, Ltd.

Replacements, Ltd. also is creating important ties with major dinnerware manufacturers around the world, including Royal Doulton, Lenox and Noritake. These have been beneficial to Replacements in procuring patterns that have been more recently discontinued. The manufacturers enjoy doing business with Replacements because it provides them with an immediate venue for their out-of-production merchandise.

"There was a time when many manufacturers would not even talk to us because, quite frankly, they didn't know what to make of our company. Now, however, when representatives from these companies come in and see the size and scope of our operation they want to do business with us," says Page.

The magnitude of Replacements' ever-growing operation is apparent when you visit the company's newly-expanded office/warehouse complex. At 225,000-square-feet, or the size of four football fields, the facility houses an 8,000-square-foot showroom and nearly $70 million worth of retail inventory.

Replacements currently employs over 300 people, more than double the number from just four years prior. Page says most employees come to the company without any specific background in tableware. "Everyone receives on-the-job training. Since what we do is so specialized you really can't go out and find experienced people. "However," Page insists, "our employees are truly committed to extraordinary customer service, a trademark of Replacements' commitment to its customers."

Most employees are cross-trained to work in other areas of the company. When needed, Page himself picks up a phone and takes sales calls. "We look for flexibility in the people we hire. We have to have team players to keep the company running smoothly," says Page.

Providing customers with the best possible service is the top priority at the company. "Customer service has really been the key to our success. We want our customers to be happy, not only so they'll come back to us but also so they'll tell their friends about us," says Page. The company offers a 30-day guarantee on all merchandise ordered. If within that period, a customer wishes to return the merchandise, he or she can do so at Replacements Ltd. expense and receive a full refund.

Over the years, a real source of joy for Page has been the many letters his company has received from satisfied customers. Most of the letters have a similar tale of a long search that ended with the discovery of Replacements, Ltd.:

"The three boxes of Ridgway's 'Oriental' china arrived in very good shape. Your company did an excellent job of packing; not one piece was broken. It's a real delight to be using dishes my grandmother had, and to have enough of them to set the table. This Thanksgiving we can set the table for the whole family with dishes that match!"
J.L., *Aurora, CO*

"I cannot tell you how delighted I am with your service, delivery, and quality of the pieces I ordered. I was hesitant to order from you since I could not believe 34-year old china from a now defunct company would ever be my china. I only wish I had done this years ago. Now our rather large family can eat from plates that match!"
N.C., *Lampoc, CA*

"I received the cup and saucer in Thun's 'Delaware' pattern and am very pleased to have it. It exactly matches my set which I purchased fifty years ago. Now my set of twelve is complete. Thank you very much for filling my order."
J.T., *Eagle Grove, IA*

"The china, Autumn Leaves by Black Knight, came yesterday in fine condition. I am so happy to have replacements. Thank you! I had nearly despaired of ever finding these pieces."
L.D.H., *Cincinnatus, NY*

Page keeps the thank-you letters in a bulging manila folder and quite often, at the end of a busy day, he'll take them out and re-read them. "It makes me feel good to know that we're doing something that touches people. We know that every set of china, crystal or silverware that we complete is part of someone's family tradition."

About the Authors

Bob Page was born April 19, 1945 and grew up working the fields of his family's small tobacco farm in Ruffin, North Carolina. He attended the University of North Carolina at Chapel Hill and graduated with a degree in business and a major in accounting. After two years in the U.S. Army, he obtained his CPA certificate and worked in public accounting for eight years. In 1978, he took a position as an auditor for the State of North Carolina.

In March of 1981, Bob left his accounting career forever to form Replacements, Ltd. He and his company have received extensive publicity and public recognition. Awards include the North Carolina Excellence Award presented by Governor James Martin, North Carolina Small Businessman of the Year, a ranking of #81 in Inc. magazine's annual list of America's fastest-growing privately-held companies (1986), North Carolina Person of the Week from UNC Center for Public Television and 1991 Retail Entrepreneur of the Year for the State of North Carolina. Page is also involved in a number of charitable endeavors and currently serves on the board of the Triad Health Project (a local AIDS support organization).

Dale Frederiksen was born June 15, 1962 in Pontiac, Michigan and attended Waterford Township High School. In 1980, Frederiksen moved to Chattanooga, Tennessee to attend Tennessee Temple University, graduating in 1984 with a BS degree in secondary education. He taught junior and senior high mathematics for three years in Kansas City, Kansas, returning to Chattanooga in 1987 to teach mathematics and to coach volleyball at Ooltewah Middle School. In 1989, he joined the staff of Replacements, Ltd. as an inventory purchasing agent and later trained in the field of computer graphics, where he has created or supervised the creation of most of the images in this book. Frederiksen enjoys researching and discovering patterns that have previously been undocumented. He also enjoys accompanying his companion, Bob Page, on buying trips around the world. His hobbies include tennis, volleyball and visiting flea markets.

Other Books By Page-Frederiksen Publishing

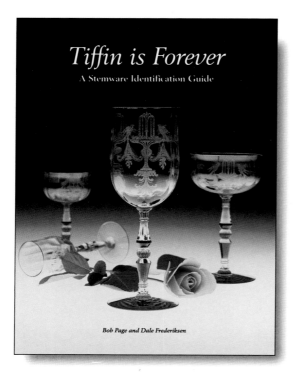

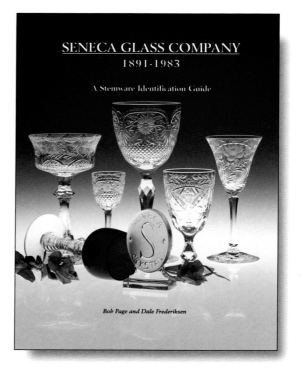

"Tiffin is Forever: A Stemware Identification Guide" (1994) This comprehensive reference guide on Tiffin stemware showcases the wide array of patterns made by Tiffin Glass from the 1920's to the 1980's. This book pictures over 2,700 stems and patterns, some never having been shown together before. This guide is a must for the glass enthusiast or collector. $29.95, add $2.00 for shipping and handling.

"Seneca Glass Company: 1891-1983 A Stemware Identification Guide " (1995) An extensive reference guide documenting over 1200 stems and patterns of the Seneca Glass Company, as well as an overall history of Seneca Glass, written by glass historian Dean Six. A highlight is the reproduction of original catalog pages showing crystal stems and holloware. $24.95, add $2.00 for shipping and handling.

Other Identification Guides From Replacements, Ltd.:

Replacements, Ltd. Crystal Identification Guide - a soft cover identification guide containing pictures of several American and European glass companies including Baccarat, Fostoria, Galway, Mikasa, Waterford and others. Designed to be used in conjunction with the Replacements, Ltd. Suppliers' Index, this guide gives a representation of many glass manufacturers. $15.00, shipping included (in USA).

Replacements, Ltd. Stainless Flatware Identification Guide - a soft cover identification guide containing over 2,000 pictures of stainless steel flatware from over 60 manufacturers. An exhaustive listing from Replacements' extensive literature with backstamp information and descriptions. Intended for use with the Replacements, Ltd. Suppliers' Index. $20.00, shipping included (in USA).

All books are available from:
Replacements, Ltd.
1089 Knox Road, PO Box 26029
Greensboro, NC 27420
1-800-562-4462